Trading the Trends

By:

Fred McAllen

Contents

Trading the Trends 5
   Introduction 5
Chapter 1 9
   Market History 9
Chapter 2 19
   The Big Picture 19
   The Hidden Market 21
Chapter 3 28
   The Predictable Market 28
   The Market Discounts Everything 30
Chapter 4 34
   The Three Trend Market 34
   What causes these trends? 39
Chapter 5 47
   Market Phases 47
   The Limited Market 58
Chapter 6 61
   The Trend and the Channel 62
Chapter 7 72
   Support and Resistance 72
Chapter 8 80
   Primary Trends 80
Chapter 9 95
   Secondary Trends 95
Chapter 10 103
   The Three – Five Market 103

©Copyright McAllen Publishing

Chapter 11	114
Entering a Trade	114
Chapter 12	128
Placing the Trade	128
Stop Losses	131
Chapter 13	135
Managing the Trade	135
Chapter 14	154
Sold Out	154
Making the Trade	161
Trade review	167
Chapter 15	170
Trading Sideways	170
Chapter 16	180
The Stinking Market	180
Chapter 17	194
Trading the Downtrend	194
Chapter 18	217
The Options Experience	217
What are Options	219
Options Pricing	222
Chapter 19	232
The Power of Options	232
Chapter 20	239
Trading the Trend with Options	239
Chapter 21	251
The Option Protection	251
Selling Call Options	257

©Copyright McAllen Publishing

Trading the Trends 4

Chapter 22 266
　The Option Spread 266
Chapter 23 272
　Trading the Secondary 272
Chapter 24 281
　Growling Bull Strategy 281
Chapter 25 297
　Averages, Oscillators, & Trinkets 297
Chapter 26 304
　Your Strategy 304
Conclusion 315

> "Financial analysts and investment advisers tend to take the market and themselves too seriously. They spend a large part of their time trying, valiantly and ineffectively, to do things they can't do well."
> ~Benjamin Graham

©Copyright McAllen Publishing

Trading the Trends

Introduction

*"The greatest investors, traders, and speculators of all time have one thing in common.
They understand the market does not always go up, they recognize the market moves in trends and cycles, and they capitalize on that knowledge."*
~Fred McAllen

Understanding how the stock market trends and cycles work is paramount to the success of every individual trader and investor. Experiencing the losses of the past does not have to repeat itself over and over. By recognizing the changes in trends as they are occurring, the trader and investor can protect and preserve their capital while profiting in any market environment.

©Copyright McAllen Publishing

Trading the Trends

To give the investor and trader the most comprehensive learning experience, this book encompasses the actual trading decisions and strategies used in both up and down markets. Bear market and sideways market strategies are traded, including trading the bull market beginning in 2009 and exiting at the highs in 2011. The decisions for each entry and exit are shared in detail to give the investor and trader a broad understanding and valuable knowledge for future market cycles.

We've all heard about the most memorable moments in stock market history like the great market crash in 1929, Black Monday crash in 1987, the brutal bear markets in 1973, 2001, 2007, and many others as well. Many investors experienced the most recent of these events firsthand.

But what is missing from these moments in history is what the market was doing just before each of these events occurred. Each time, the market gave early warning to those who listened, and the best traders and investors acted on those warnings to reap the returns and avoid drastic losses.

It doesn't matter if the next event to happen turns out to be a major market correction, a bear market, or an upturn leading to a new bull market run. The key factor is when the market begins to move in either direction there are plenty of early signs for the astute investor or trader to recognize.

By understanding how the market sends the warning signs, listening to what the market is saying, and interpreting it correctly, the individual investor can then safely enter or exit at times of very low risk with the potential for high return.

©Copyright McAllen Publishing

Trading the Trends

With the tools, strategies, knowledge, and trading experiences shared in this book, the individual investor and trader will learn to recognize the market changes early as the thoughts of the trader are explained in detail. These decision processes are explained as the market changes are occurring. And as the investments, trades, and strategies change with each market cycle, the entry and exit of each trade and investment become another learning experience.

To some, the up and down cycles of the market seem random, or haphazard, and believe its actions cannot be predicted or explained. This is simply not the case. This book will illustrate how profitable opportunities present themselves and protection of investment capital from devastating losses can be easily recognized. This knowledge will make the landscape of the trading and investing world much clearer.

The knowledge I've gained from experience and the understanding of the market have provided valuable lessons and tools to enable the individual investor and trader to become successful.

These experiences are shared throughout the book and are explained as the decisions are made.

You will learn:

- Market knowledge to enable grasping the big picture
- Technical analysis as it is used in finding entry and exit points for every investment or trade
- How to recognize market changes and capitalize on those changes

©Copyright McAllen Publishing

- Defined rules to follow in deciding to enter or exit a trade or investment
- Strategies to protect your capital at all times
- Strategies to make money in trending markets and market declines

As an active investor and trader, it is my goal to give the individual investor every tool necessary to make their own investing and trading decisions while adhering to simple and successful time-tested techniques.

You will learn to make good, informed decisions for entering an investment or trade, how to manage it, how to find the lowest risk opportunities, and how to protect your capital at all times.

You will learn many successful strategies in this book, and those strategies will change as each market environment changes. This experience will enable you to recognize future market trends and cycles and prepare you in your quest for stock market and investing profits.

~Fred McAllen

Chapter 1

> "Most losses in the stock market can be traced to the average speculator's persistent disregard of the lessons of the past."
> ~Jesse Livermore

Market History

Trend Trading

Why in the world would anyone want to *Trade the Trends?* We've all heard the sales pitches that claim the market has averaged a 10% per year return for the past 70 years, 80 years, or whatever. Sure it has. Just look at a stock chart of the past 70 or 80 years and it's easy to see. So why bother with trend trading when all you have to do is buy-and-forget.

It sounds simple. If you had invested in good quality investments 50 or 60 years ago and held them for long periods of time, then you would now be independently wealthy. That is, if you didn't buy and hold Edison Records, TWA, UAL, Bethlehem Steel, Enron, or Polaroid. And even if you avoided these companies and hundreds of others that went bankrupt, you might be too old to enjoy your wealth, have one foot in the grave, or may already be there. But hey, rest assured, or rest in peace, your heirs will be most appreciative if you were fortunate enough 50 years ago to make wise investment decisions.

Investment firms and their ever-expanding sales force consistently encourage the investor to just buy-and-hold. They make it sound so simple, especially considering that common retirement planning scenarios all promise if one just puts a few eggs in a basket, then 20 years later a chicken farm will magically appear.

Buy and Hold

Although theoretically sound and well intentioned, the buy-and-hold strategy is very difficult for investors to apply. Why? It is a little like telling someone that the way to walk from Los Angeles to New York is simply to put one foot in front of the other until you arrive. You can't argue with the instructions, but can anyone really do it? The formula omits too many important details.

For instance, during a long term bull market like the one from 1982 to 2000, the buy-and-hold philosophy worked well. But during long-term trading range markets, it does not. The basic concept behind buy-and-hold is the idea that when investors try to jump in and out of the market, more often than not, they buy at the top and sell at the bottom. This is likely true when the investor has no market knowledge and has no trading and investment plan.

Trading the Trends

But a wise investor has trouble with buy-and-hold because they know the perils of waiting to see what happens. As simple as most investment salespeople would like it to sound, it's just not that simple. Why? Because the market does not always go up, at times it goes down, sometimes severely, and other times it goes nowhere. But fortunately, history does repeat itself. And it becomes clear by taking a closer look at market history.

When viewing a chart of the Dow Jones Industrial Average for the past 100 years, from a birds-eye view the first thought that comes to mind is, "just buy and hold" and eventually you'll make money. Although some would like you to believe that, it's not necessarily the case. Take a look at the chart from 1900 to 2008 below.

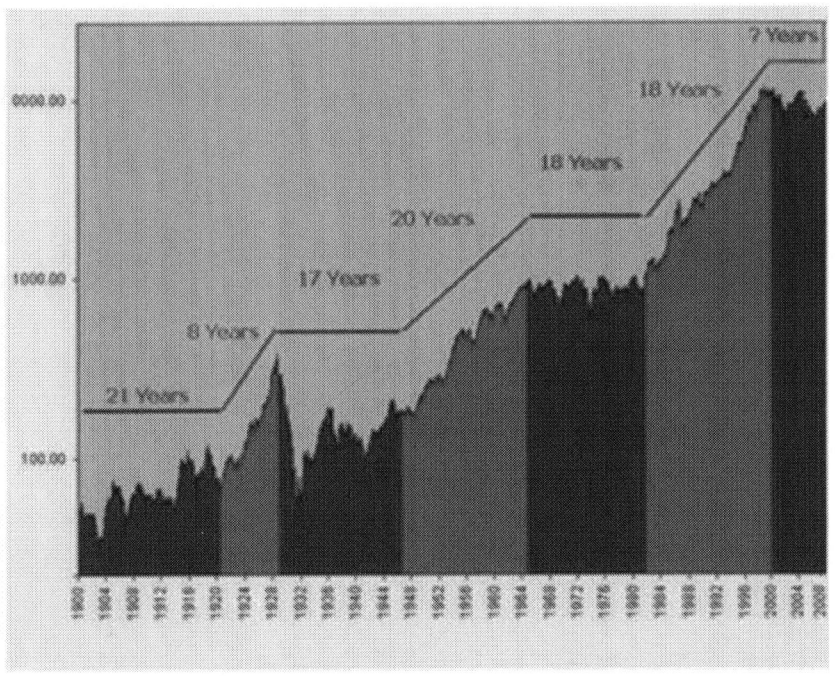

©Copyright McAllen Publishing

Trading the Trends

The preceding historical chart is very telling. Although for more than 100 years the market has advanced, there were long periods of time it did not. The investors who bought in 1929 waited 25 years just to break even. The market did not trade above the highs of 1929 until the mid-1950s. The investors who bought in 1964 waited 18 years to see a profit while watching their investments decline through numerous bear markets during that 18-year span. Obviously hoping they would someday get back to break even. What about investors who bought in 2000 or 2007? Who knows when they might realize some profit! So buy-and-hold is not that simple.

Even though the overall movement of the market has been up for more than a century, our average lifespan is less than that, and our best earning and investing years are just a fraction of a century. Other very important facts regarding market history include:

1. Since 1900 there have been 29 bear markets. There has been a bear market on the average of every 3 ½ years with the average decline of 30%. Therefore, most every decline shown on the preceding chart is a result of a bear market. Yes, even in times of long-term market advances, there are bear markets.

2. Financial advisors show a historical chart proclaiming the market always goes up, insinuating that all you have to do is just buy-and-hold, and eventually you will make money. Complete nonsense.

©Copyright McAllen Publishing

3. When looking at the chart, every long-term advance is a Secular Bull Market, and every long-term sideways or decline is a Secular Bear Market. One has always followed the other.

4. The long-term advance from 1982 to 2000 is not a normal market move.

No, the long-term market advance that ended in 2000 was not normal. Especially since the only other time in more than 100 years the market made such a dramatic advance was prior to the 1929 crash.

Yet, many of today's financial advisors and planners have little knowledge of market history and continue to advise clients based on a misguided assumption that that era (1982-2000) was normal. The most compelling explanation for the drastic market advance from 1982 to 2000 is the earning and investing years of the baby-boomer generation. See the stocks versus population chart below.

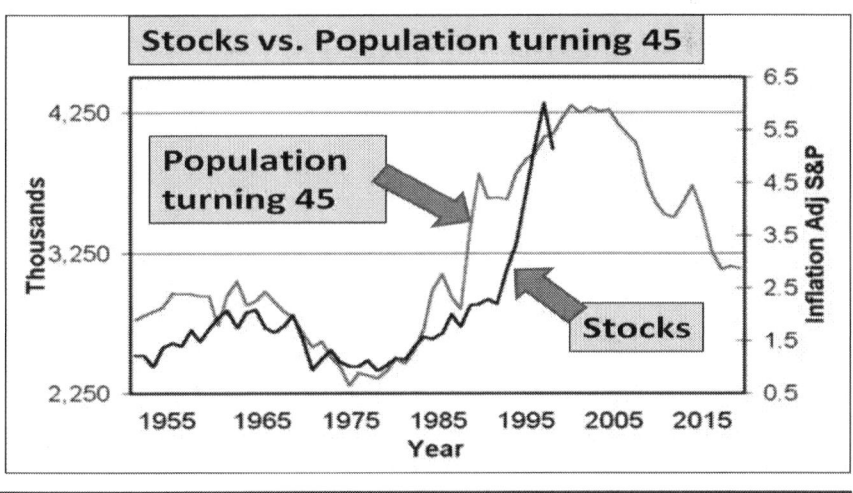

Many factors played a part in that advance such as internet and technology, opening the market to online trading, etc. But technology advances are not something new.

During the past 100 years we have seen everything from FM radio and television to space shuttles. During those times of new inventions and products being introduced to the public, the market held true to the patterns of the past. Meaning, the long-term secular bull and bear markets continued and even the advances remained more normal and methodical.

The correlation between the advance of the S&P 500 and the baby boomers is telling. As the baby boomer generation entered their best earning years and began investing for retirement, the dramatic market advance followed close behind. One can reasonably assume these same investors have begun to take money out, and will continue pulling money out of the market for retirement purposes. So I would be very surprised to see another market move like that (1982-2000) in my lifetime.

Market history also teaches us that major market corrections, and more specifically bear markets, happen more often than most people think. The problem is, most investors do not plan for the next one, anticipate its arrival, or remember the devastation of the last one. Pretending it won't happen again does nothing to protect against it. And as the saying goes, "those you do not learn from history are bound to repeat it."

Bear markets:

- Since 1900 there have been 29 bear markets
- Average decline of 29%
- Lasted an average of 1.7 years (time in decline)
- Average time to return to break-even is another 1.9 years
- Bear Markets consumed 32% of that time
- Getting back to break-even took another 44% of that time
- Only 24% of that time was spent in net gain - Bull Market territory

That sheds a whole new light on *Trading the Trends*. Since there are no risk-free investments, it makes absolutely no sense to put 100% of your investment dollars at risk 100% of the time when the market is only in net-gain territory 24% of the time.

The wise investor knows with 100% certainty he/she will be hit with a 30% or more loss if they hold through the next bear market, not to mention other severe market corrections that are just not so severe that they reach the 25% decline to be classified as a bear market. And we shouldn't forget the 2001-2004 and 2007-2009 bear markets resulted in much more than the average 30% decline. Those buy-and-hold investors got closer to a 50% investment haircut.

Now, if you listen to the soothsayers, naysayers, and other less informed members of the investing crowd they'll tell you it can't be done. They'll say moving your money in and out of the market won't work. They'll say you have to stay fully invested because the market has always produced a 10% return on investment.

Mind Bender

When someone says the stock market has averaged a 10.5% return for 70 years... that reminds me of a question posed to a group sitting at a table in a coffee shop a few years ago. And everyone at the table, including me, failed to answer correctly. An old gentleman asked:

"If a car goes a half a mile at 30 miles an hour, how fast does it have to go the second half-mile to average 60 miles an hour for the whole mile?"

After a bit of arguing between us, we all agreed that it had to be 90 miles an hour. The old fellow said, "No. In fact it can't be done. Sixty miles an hour is a mile a minute. The car has already used up a minute traveling the first half-mile at 30 miles an hour. To average 60 miles an hour the car would have to travel the final half-mile in zero time." Most of us had quickly concluded, and embarrassed ourselves by arguing that 90 miles an hour would do the trick, but he was right.

But this story leads us to a less complicated but similar question regarding stock prices.

The long-term average gain in stocks (the S&P 500) since 1928 is just about 10.5% per year. However, during the bull-run from 1980 to 2000, the S&P 500 averaged a gain of approximately 16% per year.

Trading the Trends

So let me ask a similar question:

If the stock market averaged 16% per year for 20 years, what does it have to earn over the next 20 years to average 10.5% over the full 40 years?

If we do the simple calculation, the market has to average about 5% return per year over the next 20 years to come in at its long-term average.

Take a look at the following chart and think about the long term possibilities for the stock market.

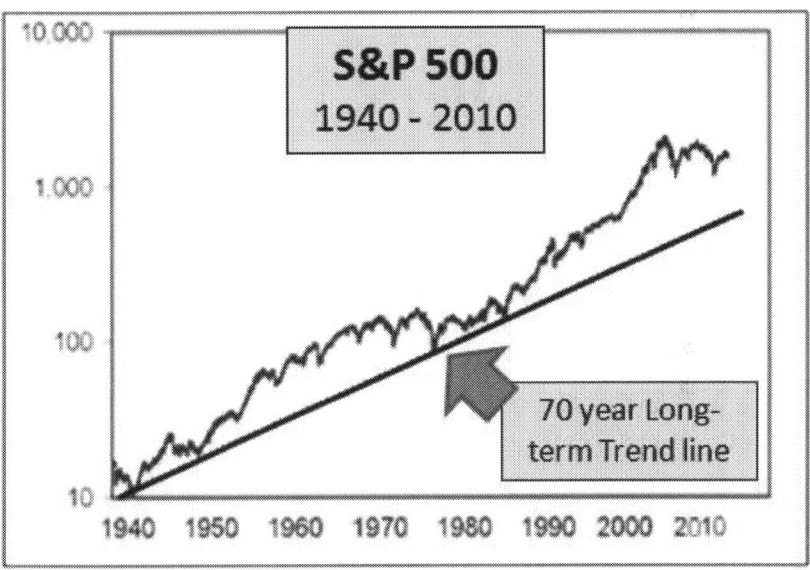

To be true to form and return to the long-term trend, realistically the S&P 500 has only two options. Either decline back to the trend line or move sideways to eventually meet the long-term trend at some point in the future.

©Copyright McAllen Publishing

Sales people will also tell you to stay fully invested so you won't miss the best days in the market. As you will learn in this book, missing the best days in the market is the least of your worries. So what if the market advances a few points today. What you really want to do is miss the *worst* days in the market, make money during the difficult market times, and protect your capital at all times.

Trading the Trends is not about trying to catch every little tick up or down like a Day Trader. We'll leave that to the folks who have nerves of steel, plenty of money to lose, and a pocket full of Rolaids. *Trading the Trends* is recognizing market trends, trading and investing with the trends, and moving to safety to avoid the losses. It is about making money during good market times, and making money when the market is declining. It's about making money on your investments when the market is not going anywhere. You know...when months or years go by and the market is in a trading range where it advances a little and then declines, taking back any gains you might have realized.

Whether you are investing or trading in stocks, mutual funds, index funds, or options, success comes by being on the right side of the market. So let's learn how to recognize the trends, how to capitalize on trends, and invest or trade with the market. Let's start with the big picture.

Chapter 2

The Big Picture

First and foremost, let's get a few things out of the way. For the most part, we are looking at the big picture. We really don't care if the Dow Jones Industrials advance 50 points today or drop 60 points tomorrow. Those daily fluctuations can be aberrations, confusing, and pretty much inconsequential to the average investor and trader.

Yes, the market moves every day. It always has and always will. Sure, the talking heads and the news writers always try to affix a reason for the move, or explain in some misguided mindless way why the market may have reacted to one thing or another. That's noise and nothing but noise. We don't care if some leader of a third-world country woke up this morning with gas pains, intestinal flu, or a sexually transmitted disease leading some attention-seeking talking head to sensationalize such an event and blame a slight market move or a little drop in futures trading on the discomfort of someone you or I couldn't care less about.

That is one thing you must learn. You must create a filter. That way you can keep an eye on the news and at the same time filter out the inconsequential, not waste your time reading it, and focus on what might really be applicable to your investing goals. For instance, on any given day the news reported will include numerous stories and headlines pertaining to slight changes in the market.

By basing your investing and trading decisions on every bit of information hitting the news wire or every story a talking head gets overly excited about, you would be trading in and out of positions numerous times in a single day.

The mistake many people make is 'not seeing the forest for the trees.' By listening to the noise, reading the insignificant news, and watching babbling fools dispense their notions, beliefs, and prognostications, it's too easy to get caught up in the drama, the sensationalizing, and lose sight of what is important, the big picture.

These daily market moves are part of a much bigger picture. That's the picture we are interested in. So we must develop a filter that allows us to overlook the craziness when we see a headline saying, "Market drops due to investor pessimism," or, "Stocks advance on optimism." Many times after reading some such headline we see the DJIA has only moved up or down 20 or 30 points and the S&P 500 may have only moved 2 or 3 points. Sure these journalists have a job to do. They have to write something just to keep it. However, that doesn't mean we need to waste our time reading it.

©Copyright McAllen Publishing

What we want to focus on is the big picture, and we have to realize the market is huge. Sure it may react positively to one story or adversely to another. But these reactions are just that. Reactions.

They are a part of the bigger picture, but they are not *the* bigger picture. To focus on the bigger picture you must understand the bigger picture is often concealed by the inconsequential.

The Hidden Market

The financial news media is constantly scrambling to and fro for stories, making all sorts of attempts to present something on TV, or write the next article that will capture your attention. They consistently keep you informed, but most of the information is of a worthless nature. In any given day you will see numerous articles and stories claiming the market is going straight up and just about as many claiming the bottom is about to fall out. That's noise. Writers either have their own opinion, or are writing about something they might have heard. In either case it's just meaningless noise. Talking heads are the same way. They have to say something. Otherwise they would look rather stupid sitting quietly in front of a camera.

Realistically, the vast majority of market energies remain hidden from individual investors and traders. Insiders are forever quietly attempting to manipulate news for their own selfish reasons. Maybe to protect their options positions or maybe to put lipstick on some pig of an investment they really wish they weren't holding. Analysts raise their ratings on companies to push the stock so their trading departments can unload inventory. Operating failures and bad quarterly reports pass through accounting magic and disappear.

As a result, market knowledge has limited value unless it has the propensity to affect the bigger picture. In order for a news story to be meaningful it must pass this one important test.

"Is it fact, or is it opinion?"

An analyst's opinion means nothing. A journalist's opinion means even less. And even the opinion of a CEO means very little since there is always a vested interest in promoting his/her company. Opinions can and do change in the blink of an eye. Facts are the only things that matter. For instance, the Federal Reserve adjusts the interest rates up or down. The GDP shows a decline, or unemployment is on the rise. Facts that signal the economic cycle may be changing. Those are facts and cannot be changed or manipulated.

News can affect the overall market in the short term, but facts can affect it in the long term. Most every stock advances with the overall market. Most every stock declines with the overall market. So when we are looking at news articles and stories regarding one company or one market sector, we must decide if this bit of news really has any bearing on the big picture. We are always looking to be on the *right* side of the market. So we want to keep a close eye on the trend of the economy.

In other words, if the economy has been rosy and chugging

Trading the Trends

along in an expansion cycle, we are going to be interested in news that might indicate that cycle is changing.

Now, if you are trading one individual stock, you obviously would scan the news articles regarding that particular company to keep abreast of any changes that might affect that company's profit, performance, and ultimately their share price. Even so, the overall market, the bigger picture, is still the ball you want to keep your eye on. Remember, it doesn't matter if your favorite company is turning profits out the wazzoo, if the general market heads into a major decline, then your stock will most likely follow suit.

Just so we are clear, I usually do not recommend that an individual trade or invest in individual stocks. The risk is just too great. Having one's eggs all in one basket brings fears of nightmares like MCI and Enron instead of a chicken farm magically appearing 20 years down the road. Not to mention stable companies who haven't made a habit of cooking their books with accounting wizardry, but still watched their stock price drop dramatically and never recover.

However, I do realize there are traders who focus on only one or two stocks and actively trade them. These traders get to know their personal favorite stocks like the back of their hand. They get a *feel* for how the stock trades. Over time they develop a sixth sense for their stocks and can closely predict with reasonable accuracy how the stock will trade on a daily basis. Sometimes this intuition is even perfected to the point they know that their stock might have a tendency to trade up or down at the open every day, how it trades

Trading the Trends

through lunch time, and possibly even how it might normally move up or down at the close of trading each day.

Even so, this type of trading might work well for a Day Trader, but not so much for the average investor. Putting your money at risk in one individual investment is far too great a risk for most investors' appetite. But regardless whether an individual is a day trader or a long-term investor, the big picture is always important. And that's where we will focus our attention.

The big picture simply means that during an economic expansion, most companies are going to be doing well, if not great, and even most of the barely decent ones will also be doing something. However, during recessions, most companies will not do so well, contract with the economy, and the stock prices will reflect this contraction.

That is why during the late stages of expansion and the early stages of contraction you will notice money being moved to safer investments. For instance, in 2000 as the tech-bubble was reaching the top and about to burst, the tech-heavy NASDAQ advance slowed down and the Dow Industrials began a late advance.

Sure, the talking heads professed that the Dow Industrials were just 'catching up' with the technology sector. Those same fools also claimed the bull market would continue. What was really happening? Well, the dumb money was still buying into the internet bubble. But the smart money was

©Copyright McAllen Publishing

selling to them and moving to safety. In other words, the smart money was moving into stocks that hold their value better in bear markets and bad economic times. Companies that provide products like pharmaceuticals, staples, etc. that everyone must have regardless what the economy is doing.

The inexperienced and uninformed have very short memories, especially when it comes to bubbles, and particularly *market* bubbles. Only a few short years following the market drubbing of the technology stocks with the NASDAQ dropping more than 70%, the DJIA was making all-time highs in 2007. The babbling fools were still around, forecasting and prognosticating, claiming the DJIA would go to 20,000. Of course, the experienced and wise were once again moving to safety.

This move to safety happens because they have seen this type of market action before. They don't need the news to tell them problems lie ahead.

The move to safety can also include large funds, not just the wise individuals. This is because according to the charter of a mutual fund, that fund must have a certain percentage of their investment dollars invested in stocks, a certain percentage in cash, and a certain percentage in bonds, etc., (depending upon the fund's charter, of course).

Therefore, they cannot just sell out and go to cash. They must adhere to their percentage of investments. If they hold higher risk stock and the fund manager is smart enough to realize a market top or a bubble, then the stock portion of their portfolio is moved to a more defensive stance. Thus, the manager would attempt to limit the losses as best he/she can.

Fortunately for you, you are not bound by a charter like a mutual fund. When the big picture begins to show signs of change, you can move to complete safety should you decide to do so. As in, move your money to a money market account, draw a little interest on your capital, and wait for better market conditions or a low-risk, high-return opportunity.

So first, let's look at how the overall market consistently and predictably moves in patterns and trends. These patterns and trends have held true for more than 100 years. As you will also learn, these trends and movements are not random.

This is why diversifying will not prevent losses. When the overall trend is down, any stock investment is on the wrong side of the market and the trend. This is why dollar cost averaging or averaging down does not work.

Adding to a losing position is a loser's game. An 'averaged loss' is still a loss. This is one of the most important factors in trading and investing, staying on the *right* side of the market. To do so, you must recognize the overall market trend and invest and trade with that trend.

When trading and investing, timing is everything. No, I am not a proponent of "timing the market" because the market moves when *the market* decides to move. So using seasonal

Trading the Trends

timing strategies, or guessing when the market might move higher or lower is like throwing darts while blindfolded.

But investing at the right time is paramount to your success. For instance, buying a stock or investment during market highs like in 2000 or 2007 is nothing more than a recipe for financial suicide. That's like the guy who jumped off the cliff. All the way down he was heard yelling, "So Far So Good!"

We will revisit the 'big picture' as we progress. We will see how the big picture presents itself in living color. All we have to do is be able to recognize it, listen to what it's saying, and change our investing and trading strategies with it.

No, the market is not random. It never has been. The chart of the Dow Jones covering 108 years of trading shows how the market moves in predictable patterns, going from one long-term move to the next. These patterns and cycles are also very evident in the shorter term.

Let's see how and why the market is not random, but predictable.

> "Wall Street is the only place that people ride to in a Rolls Royce to get advice from those who take the subway."
> ~Warren Buffett

Chapter 3

> "Look at market fluctuations as your friend rather than your enemy; profit from folly rather than participate in it."
> ~Warren Buffett

The Predictable Market

Recognizing market patterns and trends began more than 100 years ago when Charles H. Dow published a series of editorials for the Wall Street Journal from 1900 until the time of his death in 1902. This series of editorials became known as **The Dow Theory**.

These editorials reflected Dow's beliefs on how the stock market behaved and how the market could be used to measure the health of the business environment. Due to his death, Dow never published his complete theory on the markets, but several followers and associates have published works that have expanded on the editorials.

Trading the Trends

Some of the most important contributions to Dow Theory were William P. Hamilton's "The Stock Market Barometer" (1922), and Robert Rhea's "The Dow Theory" (1932).

Dow believed that the stock market as a whole was a reliable measure of overall business conditions within the economy, and that by analyzing the overall market one could accurately gauge those conditions and identify the direction of major market trends and the likely direction of individual stocks. Dow first used his theory to create the **Dow Jones Industrial Index** and the **Dow Jones Rail Index** (now Transportation Index), which were originally compiled by Dow for The Wall Street Journal.

Dow created these indexes because he felt they were an accurate reflection of the business conditions within the economy because they covered two major economic segments: industrial and rail (transportation). As you can see, Dow was looking at the *big picture*. While these indexes have changed over the last 100 years, new companies added and old companies removed, the theory still applies to current market indexes.

Learning the movements of the overall market is a very important part of investing and trading. As you will learn, if you invest or trade against the market, or its trend, you will lose. It does not matter how much you love a particular stock, index, or mutual fund, if the overall market goes down, then most likely, so will your investment.

"All ships rise and fall with the tide."

That statement is very true. As the market cycles through advances and declines, all stocks are affected. During major declines there are no safe havens. More than 80% of all stocks will decline. Conversely, during overall market advances, more than 80% of stocks will advance. Even the bad ones will realize some buying interest and gains.

As we look at the overall market, the information needed to make informed decisions is always price and volume, and this activity shows in the charts.

The Market Discounts Everything

Even in 1900, before the world of instant news, Charles Dow believed the market discounts everything. He was right, and his belief still holds true today. This belief suggests that all information - past, present, and even future - is discounted into the markets and reflected in the prices of stocks and indexes. That information includes everything from the emotions of investors to inflation and interest-rate data, along with pending earnings announcements to be made by companies.

Based on this fact, the only information excluded is that which is unknowable, such as a massive earthquake or a terrorist attack. But even then the risks of such an event are priced into the market. It's important to note that this is not to suggest that market participants, or even the market itself, are all-knowing, with the ability to predict future events.

Rather, it means that over any period of time, all factors - those that have happened, are expected to happen, and could happen - are priced into the market.

As things change such as market risks, earnings, sentiment, and any other factors that may have a bearing on future prices, the market adjusts along with the prices, reflecting that new information. The idea that the market discounts everything is not new to technical traders, as this is a major premise of many of the tools used in technical analysis.

Yes, Charles Dow was right in 1900. His belief that the market discounts everything is even truer today, and it is done on a virtual instant basis. In our world of instant news the market is continually discounting not only the known, but the unknown and the *likely*. Today's mantra is:

"Buy the rumor – Sell the news."

We see this happen constantly. At times the price of a stock will be on an increase leading up to an earnings announcement. Good earnings are announced and the stock price drops. As all information is discounted, price and volume change, and the trends become apparent. These trends are the Trend Trader's best friend.

Therefore, in technical analysis, one need only look at price movements and volume, and not at other factors such as the balance sheet. And just like mainstream technical analysis, Trend Trading is mainly focused on price and volume.

Trading the Trends

The individual investor or trader cannot possibly know everything that has affected, or will affect, the price of a stock or the overall market. But these unknown factors are not hidden. They do show up in the charts. To use a quote from my book, *Charting and Technical Analysis*,

"Charts are the footprint of money."

You see, the news story may say one thing, the CEO says another, the company public relations department something else, and the financials may indicate a whole different story entirely. But the one thing that matters is the money at risk.

The stock's price and volume show on the chart and tell the real story. There's no way to mask, hide, promote with a news release, or put lipstick on that pig. That is the money that's *on the table*. The price constantly adjusts up or down based on all factors known, unknown, perceived, and expected. The volume indicates how many people believe that price is going up or down and tells a story of its own.

Many times we never know why the price of a stock rises or declines. Maybe it happened because someone got a whiff of a news story that has yet to hit the wires or some other unknown factor. But it doesn't matter. The price is adjusted immediately and appears on the charts. Then it only becomes a matter of correctly interpreting the information.

For instance, when a stock moves higher on low volume, that tells you there is likely a limited number of buyers.

Trading the Trends

When a stock declines on high volume, then you can reasonably interpret there are a great number of sellers. Thus, the selling interest is heavy at that price. Once the price has fallen, then an advance on higher volume indicates buying interest outweighs selling interest.

As we proceed, we will use price and volume in many of the trades and examples. These factors enable us to recognize a possible change in market conditions and see early signs of a coming change in trends.

> I never hesitate to tell a man that I am bullish or bearish. But I do not tell people to buy or sell any particular stock. In a bear market all stocks go down and in a bull market they go up.
>
> ~Jesse Livermore

> "A market is the combined behavior of thousands of people responding to information, misinformation and whim."
> ~Kenneth Chang

Chapter 4

The Three-Trend Market

As Charles Dow recognized, the market behaves in very consistent and predictable patterns. Let's begin by looking at the movements of the market. The market has three trends.

1. The primary trend
2. The secondary trend
3. The minor trend

The **primary trend** may last from less than a year to several years. It can be bullish and advancing, or bearish and declining.

The **secondary trend** may last from ten days to three months and generally retrace from 33% to 66% of the primary price change since the previous secondary trend or start of the main movement.

The **minor trend** varies with opinion from hours to a month or more. But generally they are the short, reactionary movements within the longer trends.

Trading the Trends

The three trends may be simultaneous. For instance, a bullish but minor reactionary trend can be in a bearish secondary trend that is in a bullish primary movement. In other words, the major primary trend can be an advancing bullish market but have a secondary declining trend that lasts for a few weeks, and can have an advance, or minor trend, that is bullish within the secondary trend. Yet, both of these secondary movements are within the bigger picture, the primary trend. See Figure 1 Below.

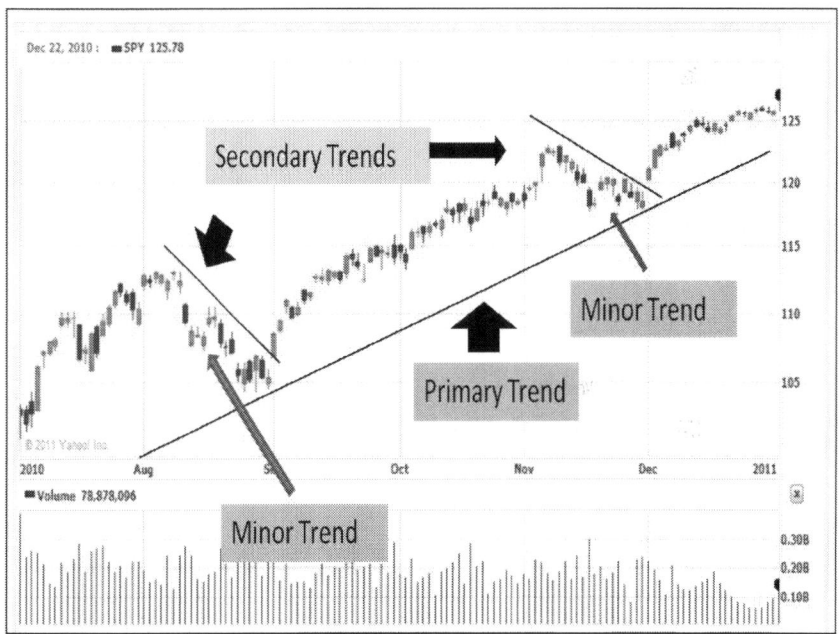

Figure 1

Each candlestick bar on the above chart represents one day of trading and clearly shows the overall advance which is the primary trend. Yet during the 6-month advance shown on the

Trading the Trends

chart, there were two secondary trends. These are often referred to as corrections, or pullbacks. And, during those secondary trends, or corrections, there were minor trends.

But these are healthy. The typical correction, or pullback, during a healthy advancing market is most generally no more than 30 to 50 percent of the prior portion of the advance. For instance, in the preceding chart the initial advance began with the SPY trading at $102 per share, advancing $11 per share to $113, and then pulling back or correcting to $105 before resuming the advance. This correction was a secondary trend moving against the direction of the primary trend, lasted about 30 days, and declined just over 50% of the previous advance.

Following that pull-back, the next advance began at $105 and continued until the price reached $123, and then pulled back to $118. Thus, an $18 advance followed by a $5 pullback, or about 30% retracement of that advance.

This stair-step type movement is classic in both advancing and declining markets. The key to recognizing this as an advance is to watch the lows and the highs. Meaning, during this advance each low was higher than the previous low and each high was higher than the previous high. The trend line drawn on the chart connecting the lows is a very important tool to use. Since during the advance each low was followed by a higher low, then the trend was up.

This trend line allows you to recognize when the trend is changing. By recognizing the change in direction early, you

Trading the Trends

can make adjustments in the portfolio or sell out completely and move your money to safety.

A declining trend is recognized in the same way as an up-trend – by connecting the lows. Let's take a quick look at a primary declining trend and the secondary trends that advance within a declining primary trend. See Figure 2 below.

Figure 2

The trend line in the above chart is connecting the lows as we did in the advancing market in the previous chart. Yet, in this chart each low is lower than the previous low which results in drawing a declining trend line.

The above chart again clearly shows that during a declining market where the primary trend is lower, there will also be secondary and minor trends that advance, going against the primary trend.

These corrections or minor rallies within a declining primary trend can last for a week or two to several months. They often raise the hopes of many investors, but until the primary trend changes, these bounces are just that, bounces, and nothing more. They are just little pieces of a bigger picture, and many times are referred to as a 'dead cat bounce,' or a 'relief rally.'

The minor trends that last for hours, a day or two, or even a week or two can be seen within both the primary trends and the secondary trends. These minor fluctuations are what traders thrive on. They attempt to catch these small moves for a quick profit.

The problem with that is the more minor the trend, the more difficult it becomes for the trader to be right. Trying to catch little swings is like trying to see a whole room by peeping through the keyhole. It's hard to do. And regardless how experienced a trader may be, he/she will never be right all the time. Therefore, a large part of their learning experience must include managing their money, managing the risks, and controlling losses. Thus, they are forever and always attempting to adhere to a formula of maintaining an average of more gains than losses.

What causes these trends?

Recognizing a Normal Market Cycle

Usually, at the start of a major advance, most stocks move up together. The pattern continues for some time. This is good, and it's the way it should be. This pattern is measured by market breadth. *Market breadth* measures the number of stocks advancing each day versus the number declining. It doesn't matter how much a stock has advanced or declined; a $0.25 advance is just as important as a $5 advance. Any stock that advances at all is an advancing stock. If the market averages are going up, technicians like to see good breadth in which the number of stocks advancing is a large number, not a small number.

History teaches us something. Usually, as a stock market advance matures, the averages continue to go up, but fewer stocks participate, which means that investors are starting to narrow their focus. A few stocks are going up a lot while many other stocks are languishing or declining a little. This is not good.

The volume of trading also stops expanding and actually starts to shrink as the averages move to their final highs. Normally in the beginning of a move, the volume of trading continually grows. But then at a certain point, the market makes new highs, but the volume contracts. This sets up a divergence between volume and price.

Another reason for market cycles is economics. There is a recession on the average of every 5.8 years. Historically, the stock market has been a leading indicator of the overall economy, thus, declining in advance of a recession and then advancing ahead of the next economic expansion. This is why we look for the market index averages to confirm each other. We like to see the overall market advance with investing and buying interest in all sectors. It becomes a red flag when we see one index continue to advance while another declines.

As a leading indicator, the market historically bottoms out, finds support, and enters the accumulation phase about six months before other economic indicators begin signaling an economic rebound and a new expansion beginning. Conversely, the same holds true when the market shows signs of topping out; this is an indicator as to what the future holds with regard to the economy.

In today's trading and investing, another way to recognize whether the indexes are confirming each other is to watch the major indexes and the stocks within those indexes. A healthy market during good economic times will experience advances in the technology-heavy NASDAQ, the S&P 500, and the DJIA. If one of those indexes is not doing well while another is advancing, this would be a red flag.

For instance, in the later stages of a bull market, the Blue Chips in the DJIA may continue to advance while the stocks of smaller companies stall or begin to decline. This tells us the flow of money is changing from higher risk to lower risk investments.

It does not necessarily mean that the lower risk investments are going to continue to advance. It only means the money is safer there. But when this happens, the indexes are not confirming each other and the divergence in the indexes can alert the astute investor of trouble ahead. See Figure 12 below.

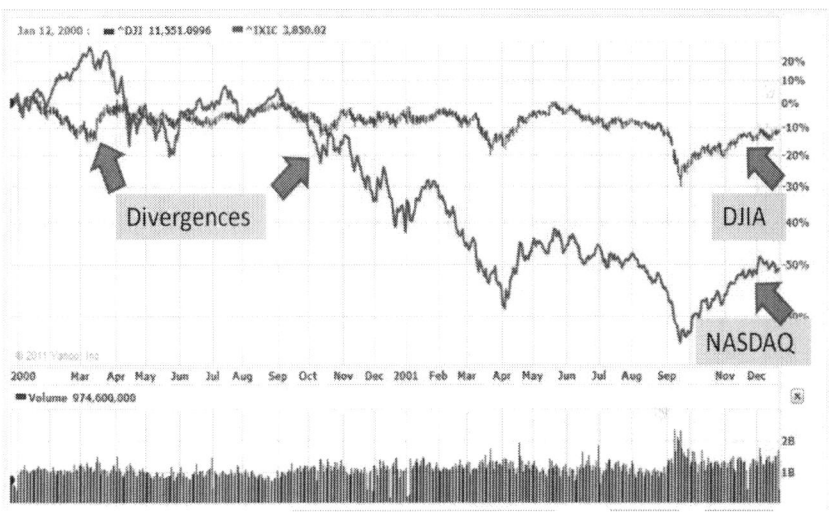

Figure 12

Looking at the divergence beginning in 2000, the NASDAQ clearly was in an Excess Phase as the internet bubble reached epic proportions. But as it began to falter the DJIA continued to hold its value. This is a typical *flight to safety*.

As the distribution phase gets underway, the Blue Chips will eventually stop advancing, but their prices may continue to hold up for a while.

At the same time, the stock price of smaller companies will continue to falter, see little or no advance, and then begin their decline. In the process of the market topping, certain events usually happen before the general averages actually stop advancing.

First, as the bull market matures, the number of stocks making new highs hits a peak number. In other words, even though the market averages are going up and continuing to make new highs, the actual number of stocks making new highs does not increase.

Second, as the popular averages continue to new highs, the *advance-decline line*, which is the difference between the number of stocks advancing and the number declining, fails to confirm (i.e., it fails to make a new high). This sets up the popular technical indication of the divergence between the advance-decline line and the popular averages.

Finally, the daily trading volume fails to expand, which sets up the third divergence. As a bull market continues, the volume of trading usually grows. At a certain point, prices continue to new highs, but the volume of trading stops growing and actually contracts. This can happen for a little while without cause for worry, but if it continues, it is usually the final important indication that the topping process is just about complete.

Thus the long-held observation that price follows volume. Where is the top? It is spread out over time and has been occurring all along at different points for different stocks.

Many stocks made their highs early, other stocks made their highs when the market made its high. Still others will make their highs *after* the major averages have peaked. The action of various stock groups topping at different points in time is the topping process. To recognize this early, one must keep an eye on the market internals.

The Market Internals

The market internals consist of the statistical measurements, such as the number of stocks making new highs or lows and the number of advancing stocks versus decliners. This information breaks down what is happening to the mass of individual stocks as the overall market moves up or down.

To understand this, remember that the market is the average of all stocks. The S&P 500, for example, is the average of the price activity of the 500 largest stocks. Everything is summarized by one simple number, but it is a one-dimensional view. When the S&P 500 is up, it doesn't mean that all 500 stocks are up; it means only that a mathematical average of the 500 is up. But there are a large variety of different market internals that can calculate to the same number. Let me clarify this.

Suppose that on two consecutive days, the S&P 500 is up 1%. From this one number both days look the same. If we went a little deeper and statistically measured what the individual components were doing, we might see a different picture altogether. Maybe on one day, all 500 stocks are up, but they all are up just a little bit.

Trading the Trends 44

On the second day, only 20 of the 500 stocks are up, but those 20 are up a lot, and the other 480 stocks are down, but down just a bit. Both days produce the same 1% mathematical average gain and look the same on the outside, but an internal look presents a completely different picture. Therefore, we always want to keep an eye on the inside of the market, the market internals.

The market internals tell us how many stocks are making new highs and new lows as the major market indexes are advancing. They also tell us the number of stocks advancing versus those that are declining. We are looking for divergences. For example, it is not a good sign to see more stocks hitting new lows than new highs while the major indices are hitting all-time highs. Similarly, it's not a good sign to see total volume contracting while prices are breaking to new highs.

If the traders and investors see divergences and believe the market is topping out, and in general has little room to advance, then a flight to safety normally occurs. Thereby selling the more risky stocks and buying the safer blue chips. This explains the divergence in the preceding chart (Figure 12).

You have probably heard the term *'sector rotation.'* This term is often used in financial news as a reason for one group of stocks declining while another group is advancing. For instance, the semiconductor stocks may have advanced more than the overall market and they begin to decline as

©Copyright McAllen Publishing

Trading the Trends

money is moved from that sector into other stocks that still have room to advance.

However, the term is often misused. Sector rotation happens constantly in advancing markets as traders move from one sector to the other buying stocks that are advancing faster than others. Sometimes it's because one group of stocks still have room to advance. This happens rapidly and would likely be *old news* by the time the average investor heard about it. It should not be confused with flight to safety.

Flight to safety is *technically* sector rotation. More risky stocks are sold and the money is moved into safer stocks. But it is not because the safer stocks have room to advance. It is because they are likely to hold their value better in an economic down-turn.

So when you hear a talking head on TV claim the recent decline in some sector of stocks is *just sector rotation*, take the information with a grain of salt. Then look at the big picture as to which stocks are advancing and which ones are declining. You might recognize a flight to safety is underway which would be a red flag you should pay close attention to. The market internals are a wealth of information.

The signs of flight to safety and possible trend change are often seen by watching *what* is advancing and *what* is declining. For instance, after a bull market run, another divergence might be the DJIA is no longer advancing, only advancing slightly, or even experiencing small declines.

©Copyright McAllen Publishing

Trading the Trends

By taking a closer look and looking at which stocks within the DJIA are advancing and which ones are not, you may get a clearer picture of what is really happening.

Possibly AT&T, Merck, Proctor and Gamble, and Exxon Mobil are advancing while other components of the DOW are possibly declining.

This information can tell you that sure, the DJIA made a new high that day, but the real story might not be so rosy. By looking within the index, you would recognize a possible trend change if the technology stocks were weak, the NASDAQ was declining, but the DJIA was stable because it was being held up by the staples, utilities, and drug stocks.

Everything is not always as it appears. It is always a good idea to keep an eye on the advance - decline line and watch for divergences. These indicators can provide insight to what is really happening inside the market.

> " Investors must keep in mind that there's a difference between a good company and a good stock. After all, you can buy a good car but pay too much for it ."
> ~Richard Thaler

Chapter 5

Market Phases

The market has three phases. These phases are just as true today as they were in the early 1900s. Understanding and recognizing the market phases is critical to your success whether you are a long-term investor, short-swing trader, a day trader, or a mutual fund investor. You always must be trading and investing with the market instead of against it. Otherwise, it will beat you badly!

Major market trends are composed of three phases:

1. **An accumulation phase**
2. **A public participation phase**
3. **A distribution phase**

Let's look at these individually with charting examples of each, as they are very important to understand and recognize.

The Accumulation Phase

The accumulation phase (*phase 1*) is a period when investors who are "in the know" are actively buying stock against the general opinion of the market. For instance, after a major decline, a market correction, and especially at the end of a bear market they are the ones who step back in and begin buying.

During these times the general opinion of the market is usually bad, and most people think it will never go back up. These are also times that some investors are throwing in the towel, selling for fear of further decline and more losses. See Figure 3 below.

Figure 3

Following a significant decline, during the accumulation phase the stock prices and the overall market do not change much.

This is because these investors who are buying are in the minority demanding (absorbing) stock that the market at large is supplying (selling). It's not that these investors are *all-knowing* and can see into the future. But most have seen the same type of market in the past. I should point out that many experienced investors wait long periods of time, maybe years, for the opportunity to buy at the bottom. Barron Rothschild once said,

> **"Buy when there's blood in the streets,**
> ***even if the blood is your own."***

Most often these astute investors have been sitting on their cash, waiting for the opportunity to present itself, letting the market come to them. That is worth repeating. The wise investors;

> **"Let the market come to them."**

Look at it logically from a risk versus reward perspective. At or near the end of a bear market, stock prices have already fallen. As I mentioned earlier, for more than 100 years the average decline during a bear market is about 30%. So at the very least, these astute investors are buying at close to a 30% discount with the risk of further decline very low and the potential reward extremely high.

Sure there is risk involved. There are no risk-free investments. But after a major decline, the risk of further decline diminishes while the opportunity for maximum profit increases. At the same time, most of these investors do not go all-in.

They test the water by buying a little, only putting a minimal amount of their money at risk, and then add to their holdings as the market conditions continue to stabilize and improve. Eventually, the market catches on to these astute investors and a rapid price change occurs. Generally, this happens after the market has likely found a bottom, shown some signs of improvement, and possibly even retested the lows from the previous decline.

The Public Participation Phase

The public participation phase (*phase 2*) occurs when trend followers and other technically oriented investors participate and also begin buying. See Figure 4 below.

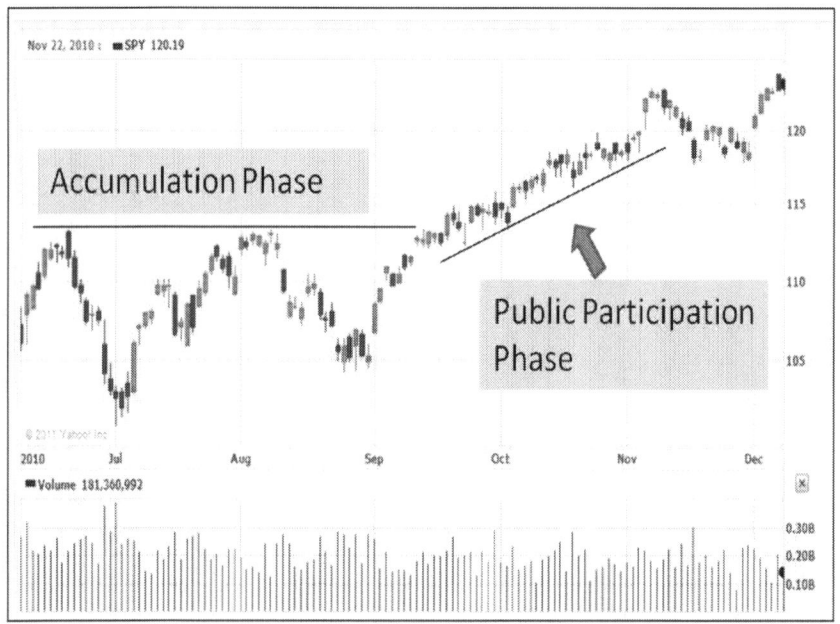

Figure 4

Trading the Trends   51

The preceding chart is a continuation of the previous chart and shows once the accumulation phase has completed, then the price advances starting a new trend from the support. More and more investors begin to test the waters, buying interest returns, and a new upward trend is established. This phase continues as the economy improves, companies report better earnings, and economic times are once again rosy. The public participation phase is a **primary trend**, and may last from less than a year to several years.

A primary trend exists until something significant proves that the trend has changed. Therefore, this market phase normally continues until rampant speculation occurs. This rampant speculation creates the Excess Phase. See Figure 5 Below.

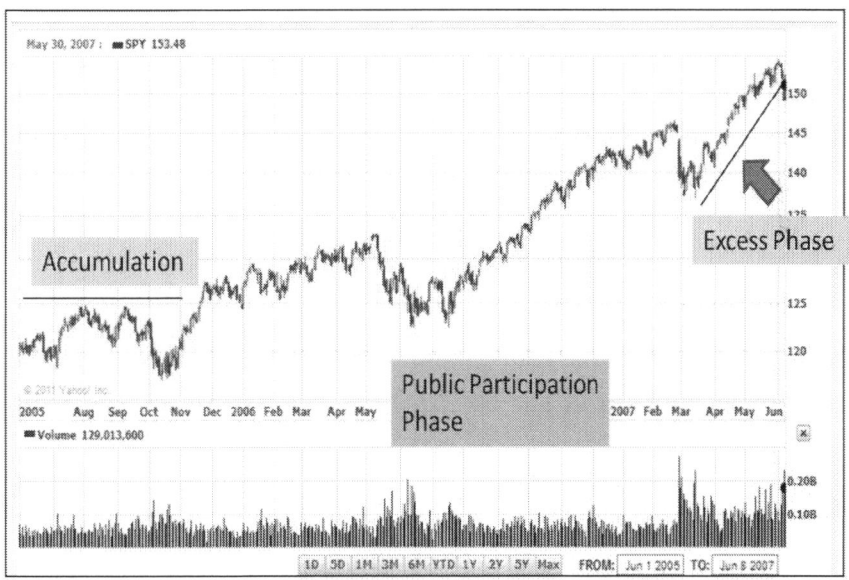

Figure 5

©Copyright McAllen Publishing

The excess phase is an extension of the public participation phase because members of the public are the active participants in the excess phase who are doing the buying.

This phase is when the uninformed, the risk takers, and the novices begin buying, hoping the advance will continue. Unfortunately for them, they are the lambs being lead to the slaughter. They are looking at the small picture, listening to the talking heads on the financial networks, and buying at the top.

This phase is liken to the tulip bubble in the 17th century or Beanie Baby craze in the late 1990s, where buyers appear ready to suspend any rational thought as they throw money into something that they desperately want. This will ultimately lead to their financial ruin.

At this point, the astute investors begin to distribute their holdings to the market and taking their profits by selling their shares to the dumb money. This takes the market into the next phase.

The Distribution Phase

The distribution phase is known as *phase 3*. This is a classic time when the uninformed investors and the novices believe the market will continue going up forever and will never go down.

See Figure 6 following.

Trading the Trends | 53

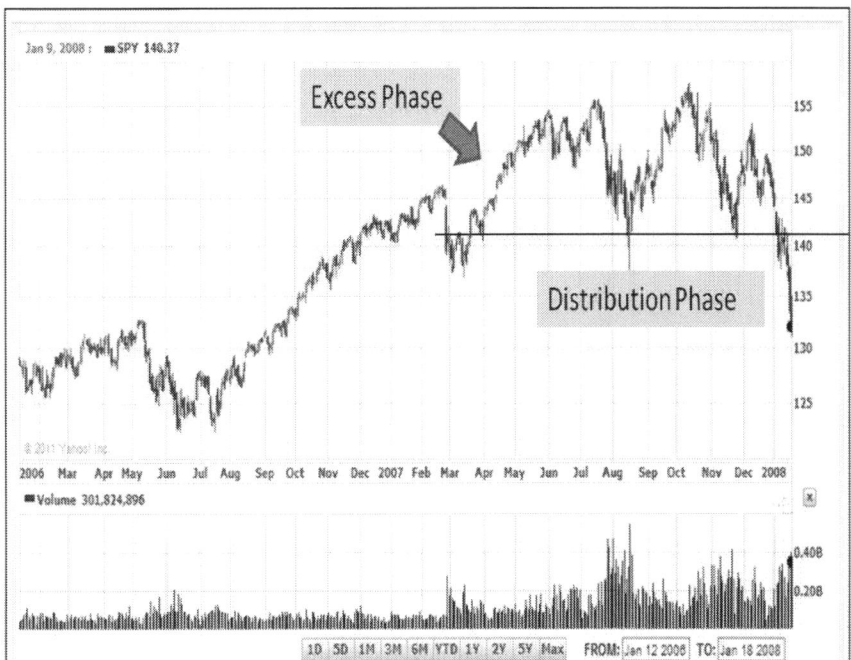

Figure 6

The above chart is an extension of the previous chart and shows how the distribution phase is a sideways move, the previous advancing trend ends, and the stocks are distributed from the smart money to the inexperienced and unsuspecting. As you should note, the volume depicted across the bottom of the chart actually increases during this phase, especially on the declines.

What does that tell you? Try to imagine the astute investors holding a large number of shares purchased at or near the bottom of the previous decline and as the market advances, they begin selling into the strength. The selling intensifies during the declines. Some may sell out completely, others may stop selling after a decline and wait for another advance to sell into. This scenario is typical of large investors.

A hedge fund for instance, might have a large holding and would be unable to sell out completely without causing a huge decline, so they sell in increments. Some sellers are actually taking a short position, selling short, positioning to capture a sizable profit on the expected decline.

Regardless of the reason or reasons, the distribution phase is simply nothing more than the smart money and the dumb money swapping hands. Obviously, this is when the money is leaving the hands of the uninformed and entering the hands of the experienced. As more and more investors and traders realize the advance is not likely to continue, the selling intensifies. It is supply and demand. After an advance, the demand diminishes and the supply increases causing the price to decline. It doesn't get much simpler than that.

The distribution phase can last from a few months to more than a year. During this phase the market will be unable to make new highs, the prior upward trend line will be broken, and a short-term sideways trend will develop. At the end of the distribution phase, the prices will falter as buying interest wanes, and prices will decline. This starts another public participation phase. Except this time it is in a declining market.

See Figure 6a following.

Trading the Trends 55

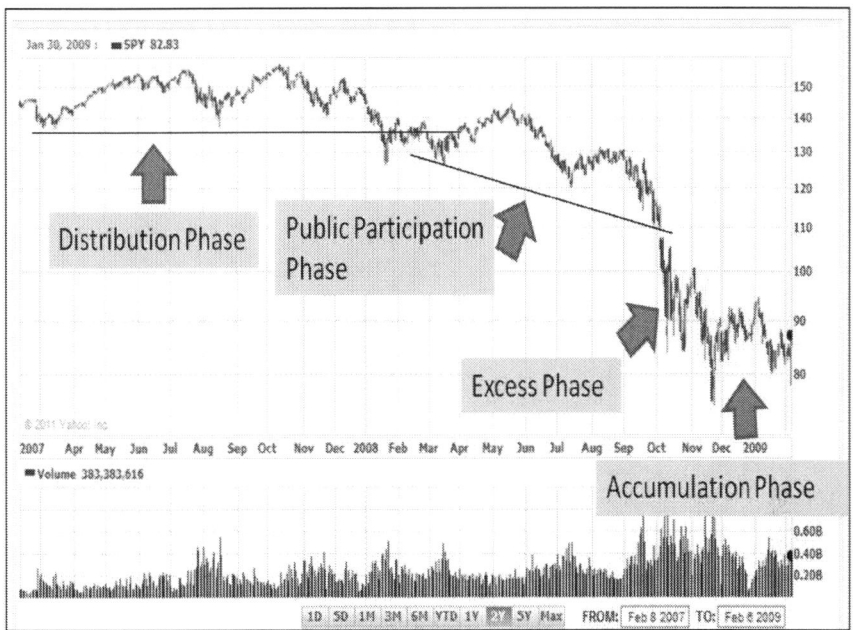

Figure 6a

The above 2-year chart is an extension of the previous chart. As you can see, this is the mirror image of the previous advance encompassing the same phases, only in a decline instead of an advance. As prices decline, more and more of the investing public begin selling as their hopes diminish that the previous advance will resume.

This phase can last from a few months to more than a year. During this time there are small rallies, but the primary trend is lower.

The excess phase during a declining trend is interesting. Most often there will be a sharp decline, and possibly several sharp declines, close to the end of the public participation phase. And these declines are much sharper than the advances in the excess phase of an advancing market. This is usually culminated by a drastic drop covering a short period of time. This is commonly known as **'capitulation'**.

Remember the novices and uninformed who were buying in the excess phase of the previous advance? Often this is the same crowd, throwing in the towel, giving up all hope of ever getting back to break-even.

Remember the astute investors who were distributing their shares during the excess phase at the top? Yep, they are back. Buying at fire sale prices when there is very little downside risk and the potential reward is extremely high.

See Figure 6b below.

Figure 6b

Trading the Trends

The preceding chart is an extension of the previous chart, moving ahead in time with the exact same security (SPY).

Once the accumulation phase is completed, a new trend is established and the public participation phase begins once more. The market has phased through these same cycles for more than a century. History repeats itself.

A Different Market

Many investors and traders see the market as simply that, just the *stock market*. They never recognize the changes in the market as it cycles through the three phases.

You see, as the market moves from one phase to the next, the perceptions change. Investor sentiment changes, and the fear and greed that drive the market and the prices change within the investors.

During the accumulation phase, stock prices have fallen, the economic outlook is usually poor, and investors are looking for a reason to sell. During this market phase all news is seemingly bad. Even good news is bad. As many are consumed with fear of losing more, or maybe all they have, the experienced investors buy at the bottom and their greed drives them to risk money when the fearful are giving up. As this happens, the volatility increases, the daily trading ranges become more erratic with wide price swings. But during this phase, it's important to note *who* is fearful and *who* is greedy.

During the public participation phase when the economy is expanding and stock prices are moving higher, the overall

©Copyright McAllen Publishing

sentiment is positive. Investors are hardly shaken when a little bad news hits the wire; they simply shake it off, continue to hold their positions, and buy more. They are looking for a reason to buy. As more and more investors enter the market, the greed and fear seems to find its equilibrium. As the public participation phase matures, many buyers start having to look harder to find reasons to buy. Some will attempt to justify their positive sentiment by discounting the importance of some bad news or claiming the bad news is somehow actually a positive for the market.

But as the market moves into the distribution phase, the attitudes and buying interest begin to change once again. Sentiment changes, and many experienced investors become fearful, cautious, skeptical, and start protecting their profits and their capital. They have seen market highs before and react accordingly. They are now the ones who are fearful of losing their profits, and this fear is generally well founded. At the same time there are others who continue to believe the market will go higher and their greed drives them to buy. So, over time, the fear and greed of the participants actually moves from one class of investor to the other.

The experienced that were once greedy have now become fearful. The ones consumed with fear and through in the towel at the bottom have now become greedy. These changes are very recognizable. When the market is reaching its highs there are hardly any news stories featuring an experienced investor proclaiming his or her fear of future market direction. The experienced quietly move to safety while others continue to find reasons to justify a continued market advance.

These changes affect the trading and investing environment dramatically. The market that's in an accumulation phase is a different market than the one in a public participation phase. When the market moves into the distribution phase it is once again a different market.

The different markets require different strategies. Sure, a buy-and-hold investor may do well during the public participation phase while a short-term trader may struggle. But these phases don't last forever. And during the distribution phase, a buy-and-hold investor is entering during the wrong market. They are entering at a time when they should be exiting. Yet during this phase a short-term trader typically finds more success, just as he or she does during the accumulation phase.

Trying to apply the same strategies to enter the market in all different phases is futile, because the same strategies will not be successful as the market changes.

The Limited Market

Trading the Trends is not trying to pick bottoms, jump in and out of trades, or being influenced by every news story, talking head, and market fluctuation. We take what the market is willing to give, we keep it, and we protect it. We have discussed the *big picture* numerous times because it is the starting point of every trade or investment.

Trading the Trends

Some have visions and fantasies of making huge profits. Most of these unrealistic ideas generated during the long-term secular bull market run from 1982 to 2000. During that time it was only necessary to buy *something*, hold it, and eventually you would likely see profit. This type of market activity created false expectations for most, especially the unsuspecting investors. Investment sales people have continued to use that time period as a sales tool when advising clients to just buy-and-hold.

But that era ended in 2000 with the bursting of yet another bubble, and a new secular bear market began. As the internet bubble evaporated, efforts to boost the economy with easy money created a housing bubble propelling the Dow industrials to a new all-time high. However, that is only part of the picture.

When looking at the S&P 500 and the NASDAQ, these indexes never advanced above the 2000 high before the next bear market arrived and decimated portfolios once again. Eleven years after the highs of 2000, the bigger picture continues to be very obvious. Secular bear markets have historically lasted from 17 to 20 years, and there is no reason to believe the current one will be different.

To expect another long-term advance like the one from 1982 to 2000 is unrealistic. As we will learn, an advance appearing on a chart that is greater than a 45 degree angle is unsustainable.

This is not to say I am a perpetual 'bear' or believe we will experience another market crash or great depression. But

©Copyright McAllen Publishing

realistically, the facts are clear. The market changed in 2000 and the likelihood of seeing another market like the one from 1982 to 2000 in my lifetime is very slim.

Therefore, **Trading the Trends** uses time-tested strategies, technical analysis, and proven techniques to take what the market gives us, whatever that might be. At times it will give us exceptional returns, but other times it will be stingy. But regardless of its mood and direction, we will protect our capital at all times, and take advantage of advances and declines when the opportunities arise.

Let's learn about trends and channels.

> "We simply attempt to be fearful when others are greedy and to be greedy only when others are fearful."
> ~Warren Buffett

Trading the Trends 62

Chapter 6

The Trend and the Channel

A trend line is one of the most effective weapons in your arsenal. It only takes two (2) lows to draw the trend. To do so, draw the line connecting the two lows and then the line can be drawn, or extended, to the infinite. See Figure 6c below.

Figure 6c

Notice in the preceding chart that after the price has made a second low, the trend line can then be drawn connecting the two lows. Although only two lows are necessary to draw the

©Copyright McAllen Publishing

Trading the Trends

trend line, the third low that reaches the line and holds above the line is further confirmation that the trend is truly in place. Furthermore, the more times the trend line is tested and holds, the more powerful the trend becomes.

The trend line gives you a very good idea as to where the stock price should find support during any corrections or pullbacks. The preceding chart shows how the price retreated to the trend line a 3rd and a 4th time, further confirming the trend. As the trend continues, your trend line might need to be adjusted slightly, but once the trend is established it should not break the trend. See Figure 6d below.

Figure 6d

In the preceding chart the trend line has been changed. When redrawing your trend line, you should always use the most significant lows. In this case, the new trend line could

Trading the Trends 64

not be drawn until there was a significant pullback to form a low.

A Trend Trader would have likely purchased after the second low was made and the first trend line had been drawn. However, any advance in the price after that point was simply trading above the original trend line until another significant low was formed. Thus, in this case was almost 90 days later.

Before we go any further you need to know why the trend line was not drawn connecting the 2 little lows on the very first advance on the lower left area of the chart. These lows are not used because:

1. The first little low was made by only three trading days, and only one of those was a negative day where the shock closed lower than it opened. Not significant.
2. The second little low was made by only three trading days. Not significant.
3. The very first advance is too steep. A healthy advance should never create a trend line that is more than a 45 degree angle. Thus, a sustainable advance should always be less than a 45 degree angle.

If you are ever holding a stock that goes on a rapid advance of more than a 45 degree angle, you should be looking to unload, *not* buy.

Take your profits and wait for another opportunity. Sharp advances are not sustainable. And you can see that the

©Copyright McAllen Publishing

significant lows in the preceding chart were each formed by about 3 weeks of trading where the price eventually declined, found enough buying interest to prevent further decline, and formed the low.

Sustainable and useful trends are formed through a process, not an event. And a process takes time. Plotting a trend line on a declining stock is also done by connecting the lows. There is only one slight difference. Stocks fall faster than they advance. Therefore the process of forming a significant low can take a little less time. See Figure 6e below.

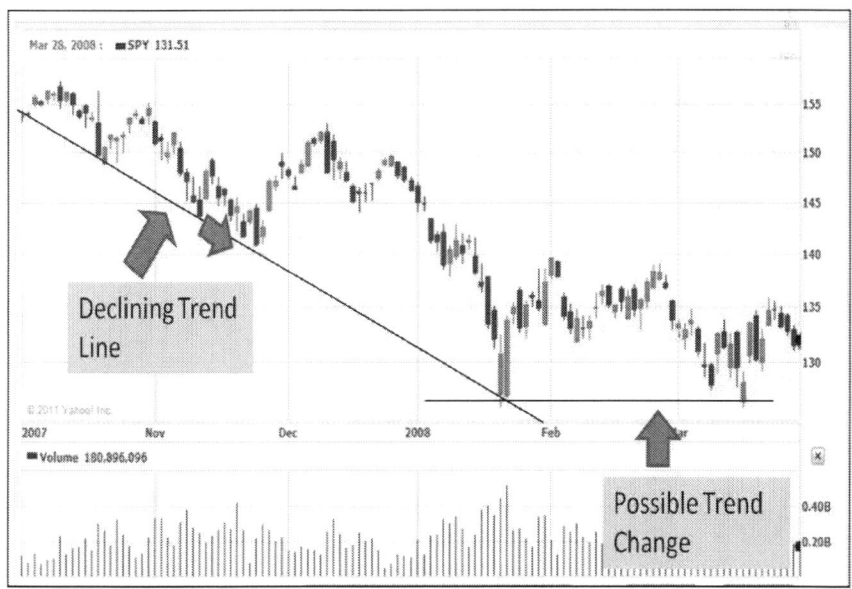

Figure 6e

Again, after the first 2 lows are formed, the trend line can be drawn. Just to point out the obvious, trend lines are an extremely powerful tool. It really is not an accident that after

Trading the Trends

a trend line is drawn the stock continues to follow that trend and find support along that line.

There are several things I need to point out about the preceding chart. (Besides the fact that it's ugly, especially for a buy-and-hold investor who is watching his/her money evaporate with every decline.) As this chart is forming, for the novice the first temptation would be to draw a new trend line from the second low at $140 and connect it to the higher low at $145 thinking the stock had reached a bottom and a new upward trend was beginning. Let's look at why that would be a mistake. See figure 6f below.

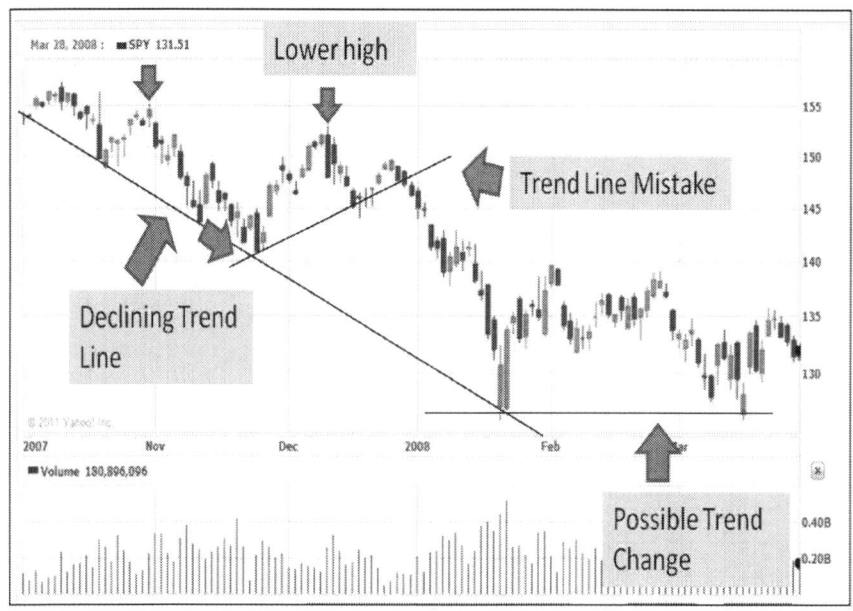

Figure 6f

As I mentioned, significant lows must be used to draw a trend line. In this case, a decline caused by only 5 days of trading is not significant. In most cases, *significant* lows are easily identifiable, such as the low at the bottom of the chart with two large positive candles forming after a 45-day decline. A significant low like that may or may not hold, but the chances of it holding are far greater.

We will discuss stop losses in detail later, but making a mistake by drawing a bad trend line or the market simply going against you is where a stop loss can save your capital. In the above example, if a trader drew the bad trend line using the $145 low and purchased at $146. A stop loss would have allowed only about a $2 loss.

That is very cheap insurance in case you are wrong.

Let's look at the top side of the trends to see how a channel line can be another great tool as well. Channel lines are drawn by connecting the highs, instead of the lows. By drawing a channel line it gives us one more bit of information to work with when analyzing either the overall market or an individual stock. We will use the channel line in different strategies and trading setups.

See Figure 6g following.

Trading the Trends

Figure 6c

Stocks trade in channels, or ranges. With each advance and pullback the channel or range becomes apparent. This is helpful for several reasons.

1. **After the first 2 highs are formed, the channel line is drawn. Then at the start of each subsequent advance we have a pretty good idea where that advance might end and the next decline begin.**

2. **We would also be alerted if an advance was unable to reach our channel line. This might also be our first warning of weakness, and any weakness might eventually lead to a change in trend.**

Trading the Trends

3. **In the event our stock advanced significantly above the channel, this would also be a warning that the advance was not sustainable and we might choose to take some profits off the table.**

The channel line on a declining trend can be equally as helpful. See Figure 6h below.

Figure 6h

A channel line during a long-term declining trend helps us keep things in perspective. A channel line serves to calm the excitement of every little market bounce, and for experienced short-term traders, it gives them possible entry and exit points for buying, selling, and short-selling. Many will wait for

©Copyright McAllen Publishing

the stock to trade higher and begin shorting the stock once it reaches the upper channel.

I might add, some traders can be very successful doing this because they understand the basic concept that a market bottom is a process, not an event. Therefore, when they see a stock trade lower and then bounce, they realize this is not the bottom. Not yet. A sustainable bottom will most usually not form as a result of one or two trading days.

Another effective use of the channel line is to alert you that a trend has either changed or is possibly about to change. For instance, in the preceding chart the stock traded in the down-trend staying within the channel until finally breaking out above the channel line. This would be a very good indication that the trend was changing.

You should also notice that once the stock broke out of the channel it then fell back in the channel but never reached the lower primary trend line. It formed the second low for a new trend line to be drawn.

There are at least 3 highs and 3 lows formed at the bottom. There were some opportunities for short term trading to capture eight to ten dollars per share.

But the most important thing you should recognize is these highs and lows were a bottoming process. It took about 6 months to materialize with 45 to 60 days trading between each significant low.

Remember the accumulation phase? That is it. It takes time. There were more than 60 days between the forming of the lowest low and the higher low needed to draw a new trend line. The point is, don't ever get in a hurry. The market will still be there tomorrow. It's not going anywhere. It does what it will and doesn't care about your investment dollars. But if you try to inflict your beliefs that it should advance, it will take your investment dollars in a heartbeat.

So always be patient. Remember, the market is huge and takes time to change from one major trend to the next. Try to think of it somewhat like the 'government.' Nothing happens quickly, if at all, and one babbling politician is not going to make any significant difference today.

So when you hear some talking head babbling on and proclaiming at the first little market bounce that "The train is leaving the station without you," just mute the TV and draw your own conclusions - and your trend lines!

> "I know from experience that nobody can give me a tip or a series of tips that will make more money for me than my own judgment."
> ~Jesse Livermore

Chapter 7

> "Reoccurring patterns occur over and over because stocks are driven by humans and human nature never changes."
> ~Jesse Livermore

Support and Resistance

A trend or channel line would be impossible to draw if there were no support or resistance. The support a stock finds when it declines and the resistance during an advance are the most important factors in trading, and they are visible on a chart in both the short term and the long term.

Support and resistance organizes the charting landscape into well-marked levels that do predict market trends, swings, and breakouts. Support and resistance may present an absolute barrier that cannot be crossed or exhibit elasticity that can be stretched but not broken. We see this at times when a stock falls through support only for a short time before returning to trade above that level.

Trading the Trends 73

Resistance can work the same way, since at times a stock may temporarily break above a resistance level only to fall back below it. We saw this in the preceding chart (Figure 6c). The stock traded above the channel line only for a couple of days and then returned to the channel.

In common horizontal support and resistance, resistance becomes support when stock price finally trades above it and remains there and vice versa when it falls through. Horizontal price marks the most common form of support and resistance. These important highs and lows reveal scarred battlegrounds between bulls and bears. See Figure 5a below.

Figure 5a

These battlegrounds carry an emotional shadow that truly has lasting influence whenever a price returns to the old level.

The preceding chart shows the support the S&P 500 found just below the 1050 level on the right side of the chart. The more times a support level is tested the more powerful it becomes.

Starting from the left side of the chart, the wick of a daily candle touched the lower support level and then the index traded higher to close that day. But that same support was tested 5 more times and only failed the test once. Even then, within 5 days the stock returned to trade above the support.

The resistance also shown on the preceding chart tells its own story. The first high shown in mid-June was tested once again about two months later and the resistance proved too strong and prevented the advance. The third time it reached that level it traded just below resistance for 4 days before gathering the momentum to finally break out above it.

Another very important fact is after breaking through the resistance, it then traded 10 days on top of that level before finally advancing further. Technically speaking, this served as a test, showing the old resistance had now become support.

Market tops during frantic rallies may persist for years and be tested many times. Failed tests at those levels reinforce resistance and generate a pool of investors willing to sell at those levels. Experienced investors who buy at market bottoms remember these resistance levels. When the stock returns to a high, they begin selling into the strength.

Market bottoms tend to draw bottom support and then test it repeatedly. Over time, these become significant floors during future market corrections and generate buying interest. Experience is a great teacher. And when a stock declines to a known support level it attracts buyers who are expecting the support to hold. These old levels can become support once again months or years later. Let's extend the time-frame on the preceding chart and see what happens. See figure 5b below.

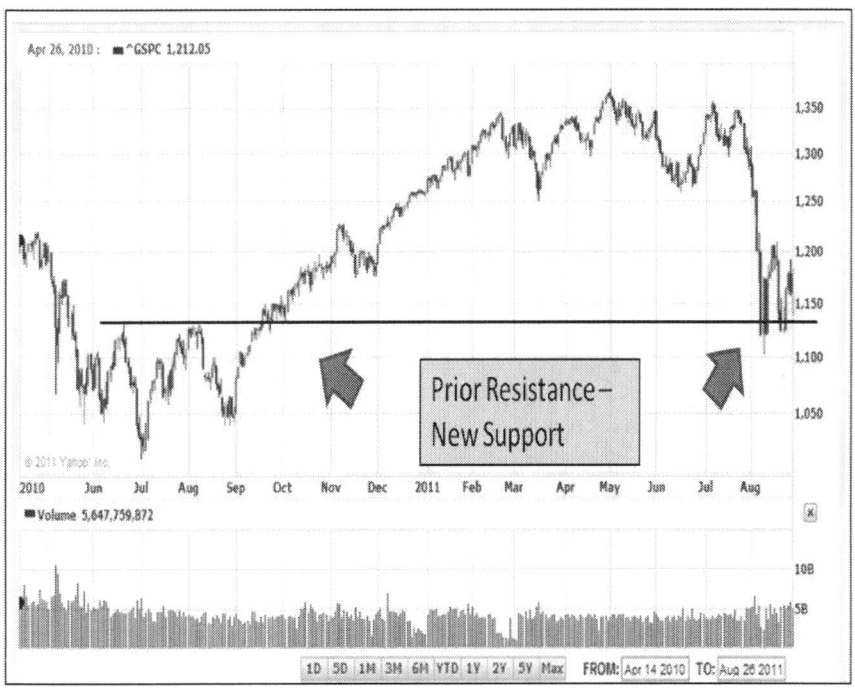

Figure 5b

Trading the Trends

Clearly, the old resistance just below the 1150 mark became support. A year later the market returned to that level and the old battlefield returned. Obviously, a failed effort by the bulls to hold that level would mean the next level of known support would be the 1050 level that was tested numerous times in the past.

Even during an advancing market, pullbacks and corrections can create support levels along the way. These levels of even minor support may be tested during future corrections.

Conversely, during a declining market, bounces and rallies can create resistance levels that will be tested in the future. One should never think these are simple anomalies that occur.

During the formation of every level of resistance or support, real money was changing hands creating these chart patterns. And logically speaking, the more money that changes hands during the creation of a support or resistance level and subsequent tests of those levels speaks volumes as to their significance.

Money talks... and it speaks very loudly. When a stock has traded down to a support level and that level holds, then there is no questioning the fact more money was buying than was selling. At a major support level, some investors stop selling to see if the support will hold. This relieves some of the selling pressure, but if support is broken then a downdraft can occur.

Trading the Trends

The same scenario applies to market tops. When resistance cannot be penetrated, then the greater sum of money was the dominating factor.

Minor support and resistance levels don't carry as much weight, but they can still be meaningful and useful.

See Figure 5c below.

Figure 5c

During an advance in 2010 the S&P 500 found resistance at the 1200 level and then took more than 30 days to finally break through and move higher. As indicated on the chart, the level was first tested in late October during a single trading day only to trade lower to close. It was then tested

©Copyright McAllen Publishing

three more times before breaking through. After falling back below resistance, on the ninth trading day it was able to move higher.

At the time, this may have seemed minor even though it took two attempts to successfully move above that level and stay. Yet from start to finish, there were about 27 trading days involved in breaking this resistance level. That is considerable money involved.

Let's expand our chart to look back and see where this resistance might have originated. See Figure 5d below.

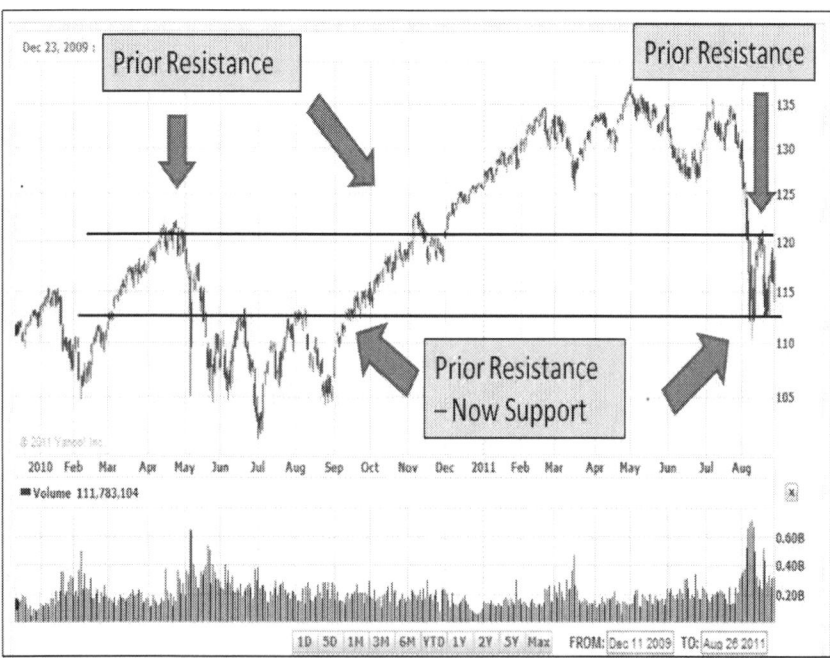

Figure 5d

Trading the Trends

Clearly, the resistance level in the previous chart originated 6 months earlier when the market was unable to move above that level. Prior resistance has now returned two more times. Although the old level of resistance offered no visible support in the near free fall as the market fell through it on the right side of the chart, it did return with the first bounce. Once again being a level that is difficult to cross.

Technical indicators do provide valuable market knowledge and can accurately predict future market movement. For instance, regardless which direction the market takes next, one can easily see on the preceding chart where the next lines of support and resistance will be.

As we progress, support and resistance will often be a large part of the decisions to find entry and exit points for trading and investing. The safest, lowest risk opportunities are usually found at or near a support or resistance level.

> "The price pattern reminds you that every movement of importance is but a repetition of similar price movements, that just as soon as you can familiarize yourself with the actions of the past, you will be able to anticipate and act correctly and profitably upon forthcoming movements."
> ~Jesse Livermore

©Copyright McAllen Publishing

Chapter 8

Primary Trends

The primary trend is the Granddaddy of the 3-trend market. **Once a trend is established, it continues in the same direction until some definitive signals prove it has ended.**

Before putting a single dollar of investment capital at risk in the market, the wise investor will know which direction the primary trend is headed. If it is headed lower, then the money should either stay in the account until the trend changes directions, or the investor should be looking for opportunities to make money in declines. Market decline strategies include short selling or buying put options.

Major trends exist despite "market noise". Markets might temporarily move in the direction opposite to the trend, but they will soon resume the prior move. The primary trend must always be considered during any such bounces or reversals.

Determining whether a reversal is the start of a new trend, a temporary movement, or pullback in the current trend is not easy. But there are tools that will help you make the correct determination. The use of a trend line is one of the most valuable tools you can use.

See Figure 7 below.

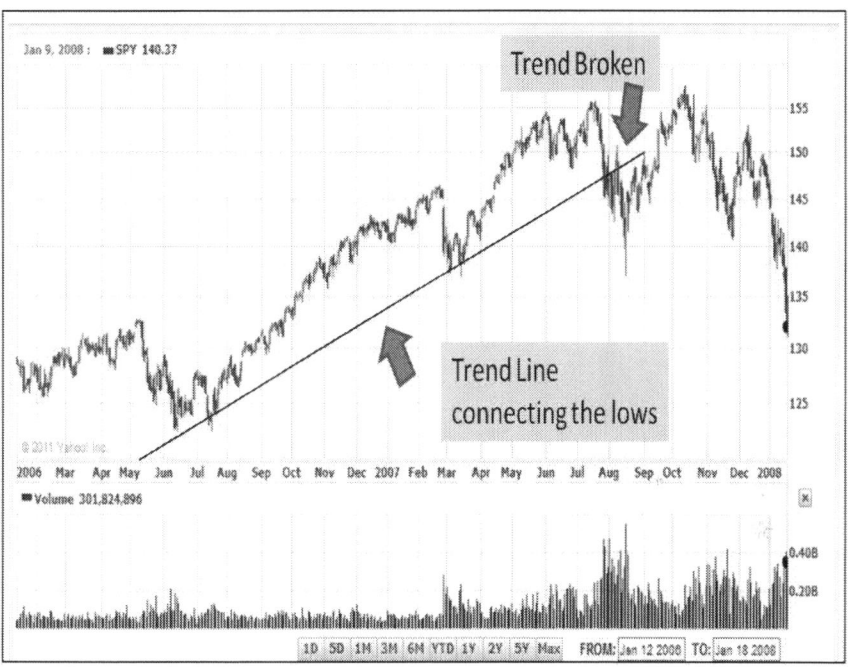

Figure 7

I have used the SPY for this charting exercise because it is one of the most reliable for overall market movement since it contains 500 of the largest companies in the world. And when you want to know the primary trend of the overall market, the SPY is a great choice.

Trading the Trends

In the preceding chart, the trend line is drawn connecting the lows. This upward trend continued for more than a year until it was broken when the price closed below the trend line. At that point, that was the very first signal that the trend may change. When in fact, that is exactly what happened. The distribution phase was underway, and a down-trend eventually began.

Let's look at how long-term trends do continue and how effective and accurate they are. First, take a look at the trend from May 1970 to February 1973 for the Dow Jones. See Figure 7a below.

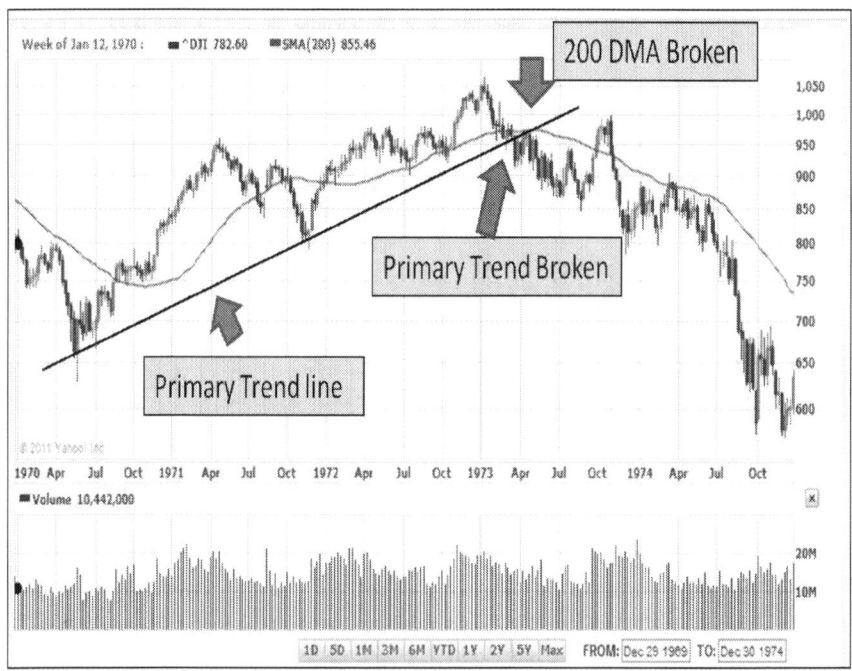

Figure 7a

The upward trend continued for more than 2 years before the trend was broken. Now look at the trend from 1996 to when the trend was broken in October 2000. See Figure 8 below.

Figure 8

In the above chart the trend line could have effectively been drawn after the second low (April 1997) and extended to the infinite. This is how powerful a trend line can be. For more than 4 years, every time the price declined it found support at the trend line. And yes, the more times the price falls back to the trend line and holds, the more powerful the trend becomes.

The fact that this stock traded above the trend line, tested it, and then moved higher is not an accident. Several factors play a significant role here. For instance, traders use trend

Trading the Trends

lines to find entry points to buy. Thus, when the price declines back to the trend line there are traders who begin buying which helps support the price at that level.

Another reason trend lines are so effective goes back to the beliefs of Charles Dow. He believed the market was a reflection of the general health of the economy. The economy is huge, and it doesn't expand overnight, or make quick moves. It takes time. And this expansion shows up on the chart as a continual advance. So, as the economic expansion continues, so does the output of companies, their earnings increase, and so does the price of their stocks.

Look at what happened when the trend line was broken in October, 2000. See Figure 9 below.

Figure 9

Trading the Trends

The preceding chart is just moving ahead in time from the previous chart.

Once the trend is broken, a new trend begins. Do you see the distribution at the top? Even before the trend was broken, the distribution had begun.

Notice that after the highest high, two more highs were made but were not as high as the first. This is typical distribution. Looking at the long-term advance, every high along the way was followed by a higher high.

This is very important to remember. When a stock is unable to make a higher high after a long advance, then that is your first red flag. The inability to make higher highs is one of the first signs of weakness.

The early distribution prior to the trend being broken is sometimes anticipatory. Some experienced investors who purchased near the beginning of that trend would be anticipating a trend change. Many would expect a major correction and possibly a bear market.

And like an old successful stock operator once said:

"I never buy at the bottom and I always sell too early."

Joe Kennedy said, **"Only fools hold out for top dollar."**

The point is, once a sizable profit has been made, you then have to rethink your risk versus reward. The last thing you want to do is watch a big profit turn into a loss while you are hoping for more profit. During the distribution phase the wise

Trading the Trends

traders and investors cut back, tighten up stop losses, take some profits off the table, and take measures to preserve profits and prevent loss.

After breaking the old primary trend, a new primary trend began. The ensuing downtrend lasted more than 3 years. This is why **Trading the Trends** is your best friend. Can you imagine the financial devastation of losing close to half your investment capital by hanging on during a major decline? But once the primary trend is in place, it does continue until broken, and those who hold on and hope during declines pay dearly.

I am sure you noticed on the preceding chart that the new declining trend followed our trend line down and the accumulation phase at the bottom began. The accumulation phase took just about 6 months. This is typical of a major correction. This is a time when the stock is finding support, buying interest is returning, and normally the economy is showing early signs of stabilizing.

This is very important. The accumulation phase is a bottoming process. A **process,** not an **event,** and it takes time. Very seldom will you see a perfect V bottom. Many times during a major decline there is no prior support to indicate when the market has reached a bottom. So never get in a hurry to buy. When investing, the one thing you don't want to try to **pick** is the bottom. There is always plenty of time to buy once the bottom has formed and a new trend begins. Now, let's extend our time on the previous chart once more. See Figure 10 below.

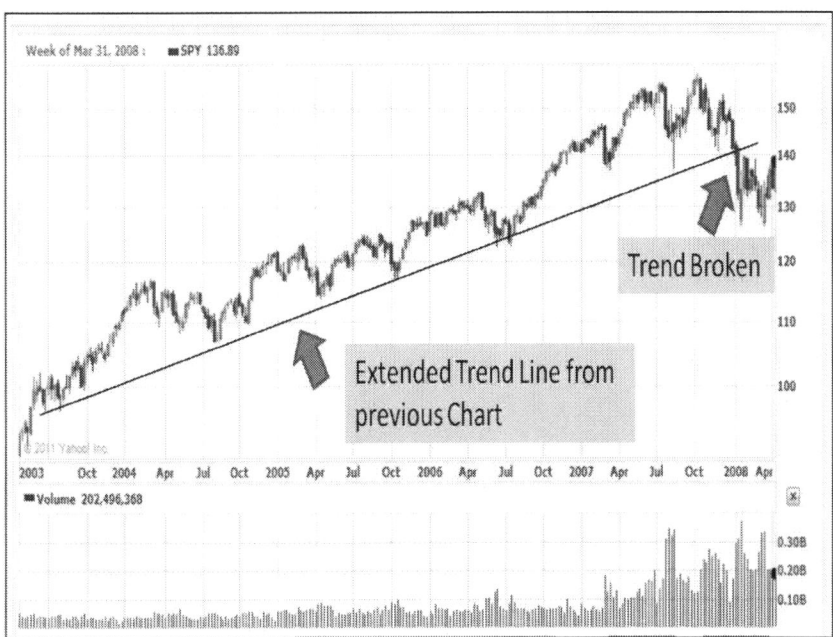

Figure 10

After the previous accumulation phase, the new trend advanced for three years or more. And once again, the trend remained in force until it was broken in late 2007.

Let's look at another tell-tale sign of coming trend change. The trading volume is displayed across the bottom of the above chart. I go into great depth regarding the technical approach to investing and trading in my book, *'Charting and Technical Analysis,'* but I want to point out something very important here as well.

In the preceding chart, during the long-term trend the volume was consistent, hardly any spikes up or down, until the late stages of the advance when the distribution phase began. Notice how the volume increased dramatically at the beginning of the distribution phase.

Now, imagine you own shares of this stock and have watched the advance for a year or more. Then you notice in April and May of 2007 that the stock made a new high on increased volume. Normally that is good. The volume should confirm the trend. Meaning, if the trend is up, then there should be higher volume on up days and lower volume on any declines. But at the top of the advance notice how the volume spiked much higher on the down days and was lower on the up days. Exactly reverse as it should be for a healthy advancing market. It is important to remember that this volume change was happening *before* the trend line was broken.

This is a tell-tale sign that change is in the air, and another tell-tale sign of distribution. An investor in this stock should be overly concerned when seeing this happen. The charts are the footprint of money. The volume indicates the buying and selling interest. When the volume increases on the declines after an advance, this tells you the selling interest is higher than the buying interest. And that is certainly not a good sign if you are holding this stock in your portfolio.

It doesn't matter what you might think about this stock at that point. It may be your favorite stock. You may think it should go higher. You may think the company's fundamentals are

Trading the Trends

sound and rock-solid. But the market is speaking, and it is the only one that matters.

It makes no difference what the fundamentals are, what the company's outlook might be, or what silly rating some investment firm might have given your stock. The best companies will follow the overall market up or down. And investment firms are notorious for raising their ratings on a company in efforts to support the stock price so they can unload it from their inventory. Never ever buy a stock because an investment firm raised their rating on it. I repeat, **never**.

Let's look at one more chart that is an extension of the previous chart. See Figure 11 below.

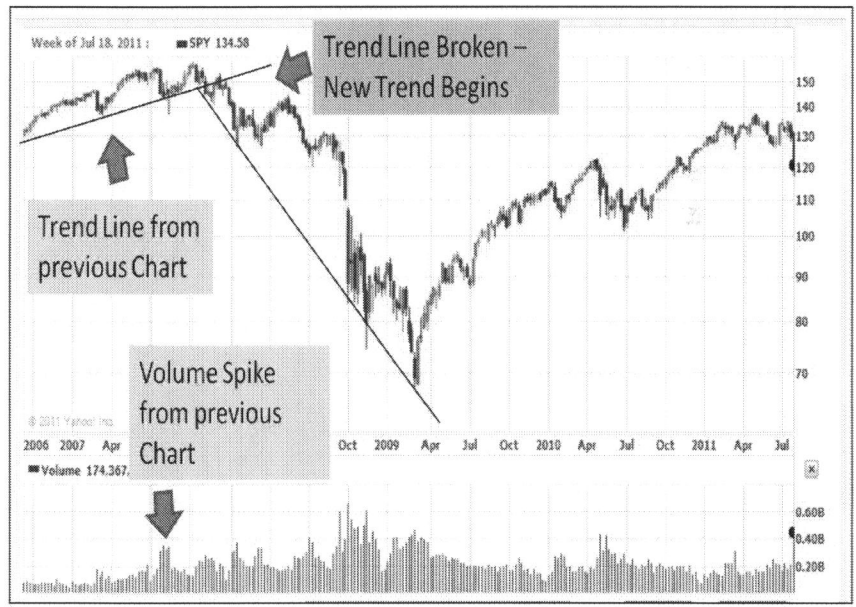

Figure 11

Trading the Trends

As you can see, the same scenario repeats over and over again. The market trends up, distribution, then trends back down and accumulates.

It doesn't matter how many charts you pull up for the past 100 years, it is the same exact scenario with every market cycle. When **Trading the Trends**, you can't predict when the trend will change, nor should you try to. But you can recognize the trend and trade and invest with it. Let the market come to you!

Primary trends do last from several months to several years. The downtrend in the preceding chart lasted 17 months and resulted in about a 50% decline. This was obviously a bear market. And since these bear markets have happened on the average of every 3 ½ years since 1900, that's a pretty accurate track record. So it is certainly something a wise investor or trader would begin anticipating after a 2 ½- or 3-year market advance. Also, for more than 100 years the average bear market decline lasted 1.7 years. This should also be considered when the market is in bear stages. Don't try to pick a bottom, let it happen, recognize it, and then invest with the new trend while always protecting your capital.

Notice the increased volume during the down trend. This is simply more money changing hands with the selling interest high. In other words, the volume *is* confirming the trend. And no, that is not a perfect V bottom. The bottoming process started with the highest volume during the decline 45 days before the lowest point was reached. Anyone trying to catch that *falling knife* and *pick the bottom* is likely to experience a very bad cut on their investment account balance.

Remember, the *trend is your friend*. Stay clear of falling knives!

There is one thing the end of every primary trend has in common, whether it's the market tops in 1973, 2000, 2007; the market bottoms in 1974, 2004, 2009; or every other top and bottom in each market cycle. That is – breaking below the trend line or above the channel line.

Each time the primary trend was broken it was the investor's early warning the market had changed and the trend was likely changing as well. With each change of direction there is a pivot point. A point when the market can no longer make new highs at a top or new lows at a bottom, and the pivot point is where the scales tip in the other direction.

The Pivot Point

The pivot point has long been discussed with regard to technical market analysis. Jesse Livermore has been regarded as one of the greatest traders of all time based on his successes in the early 1900s. In his book "*How to Trade in Stocks*," there is an entire chapter about the pivotal point. He begins by saying, **"Whenever I have had the patience to wait for the market to arrive at what I call a 'Pivotal Point' before I started to trade, I have always made money in my operations."**

Trading the Trends

For me, the breaking of a trend line on a price chart is an example of a pivot point. It represents a clear cutoff where the trend of the market has been broken or a new trend began. The reason a pivot point is so valuable is that it allows a trader to know when a trade is wrong with the least amount of loss or is a signal to a long-term investor the market is changing.

This is especially true if the trade is longer term. Suppose the market has been down and then moves up and threatens to break above a long-term channel line. It then breaks through and moves up on expanding volume. The investor takes a position. The odds are that the market might pull back, but if the advance is the real thing, it should not break below the line again.

If it does, one should sell out with a small loss. If it does carry through as expected, one has entered into a long-term trade at a very favorable starting point, and done it with very little risk. If the market fails and the loss is taken, the investor must understand that here was an opportunity to make a large gain, and he/she tested the waters with minimal loss. This time it was a loss; the next time probably won't be.

Remember that any trade is only one trade in what may amount to a thousand over time. Don't ever put everything, either mentally or emotionally, into a single trade.

I have observed something about pivotal points on and off for many years. It is this: At times the stock market can become

©Copyright McAllen Publishing

very indecisive. Volatility dies down, and the market seems to lack direction. As this continues, more and more people start noticing the lack of direction. This lack of direction will usually manifest in all three trends – short, intermediate, and long term.

When that happens, you notice that everyone starts looking at shorter and shorter price moves to resolve the indecision, or they look with a microscope at an impending news item to resolve the uncertainty. When an announcement comes in, the response is normally huge, as investors take the result as a resolution of the indecision. It seldom is.

Beware when it seems that all of Wall Street is looking at one short-term event or one news item to tell them what is going to happen long term. These widely agreed-to pivot points are seldom the real ones. When looking for market pivot points, changes in trend, market tops, or market bottoms, you should think logically. When the market tops out, falls through a primary trend line and a long-term moving average, there is a reason for this movement.

After such a decline, many traders and investors want so badly for the market to continue advancing that they find hope and encouragement on the first bounce. Take a look at the following chart, Figure 11-1.

Trading the Trends

Figure 11-1

In the above chart the QQQ fell below the 200 DMA in May, 2011, and then in August it fell once again. The last decline was sharp and severe. Yet, after about a 10% decline from the top, the first bounce gains back about 40% of the decline.

Logically, what changed? The economic conditions, market weakness, or any factor causing the substantial decline were still the same. Nothing significant changed in one week. The pivot point was the breaking of the primary trend line and breaking below the 200 DMA. No, the bounce will not result in a return to the market highs any time soon. It's just a bounce.

Chapter 9

Secondary Trends

The second of the 3-trend market is the secondary trend. It may last from ten days to three months and generally retraces from 33% to 66% of the primary price change since the previous secondary trend or start of the main movement.

In order to recognize a secondary trend you must first plot the underlying primary trend. We do this in the following example by connecting the lows on a 1-year chart. See Figure 11a below.

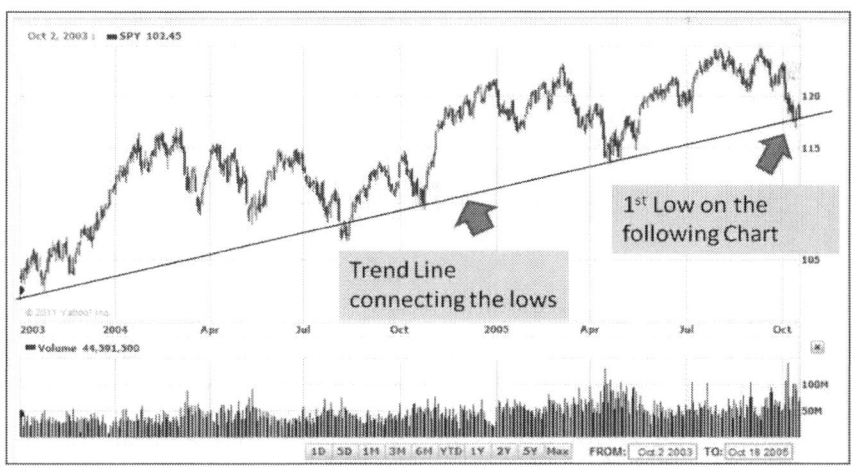

Figure 11a

You should be aware that the secondary trends very often are significant corrections, or pullbacks, such as these and are ultimately the ones used to draw the trend lines on the long-term charts. As an example, notice the last low on the preceding chart is the October low and is in fact the first low on the following chart. See Figure 11b below.

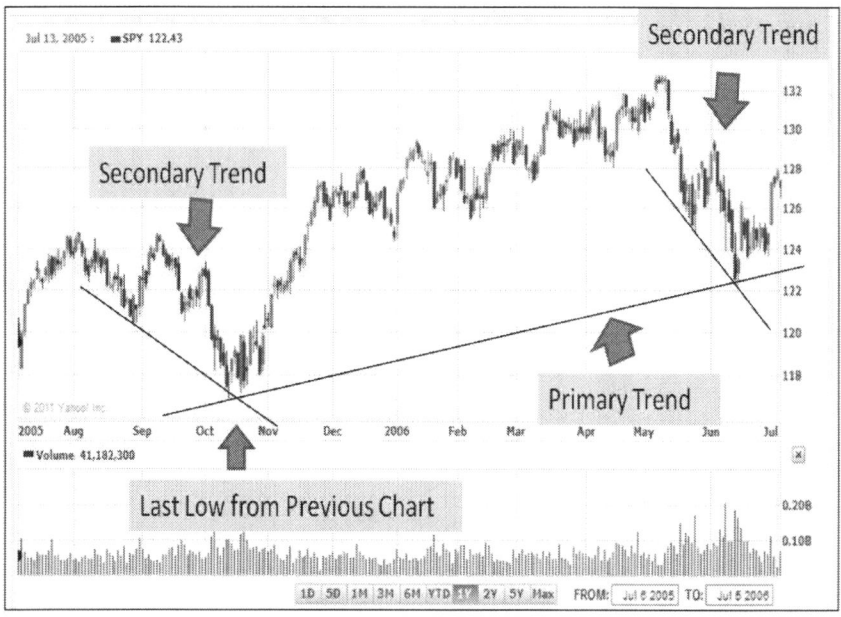

Figure 11b

By using two charts you can see there were significant secondary trends on the previous chart (Figure 11a) and there are two more on the above chart (Figure 11b). These secondary trends are simply periods of decline within an advancing primary trend. In the above chart, the first secondary trend traded against the primary trend for 2 ½ to 3 months before resuming the advance and the second declined for almost 2 months before resuming the advance.

Each of these secondary trends created a drop in the share price of about 8 to 9 percent. We will discuss trading secondary trends later, but the above example is why many short-term traders attempt to trade these medium range trends. Simply, they can capture a nice profit and sit on the sidelines with no capital at risk until another opportunity arises. Secondary trends also appear during a declining primary trend. See Figure 11c below.

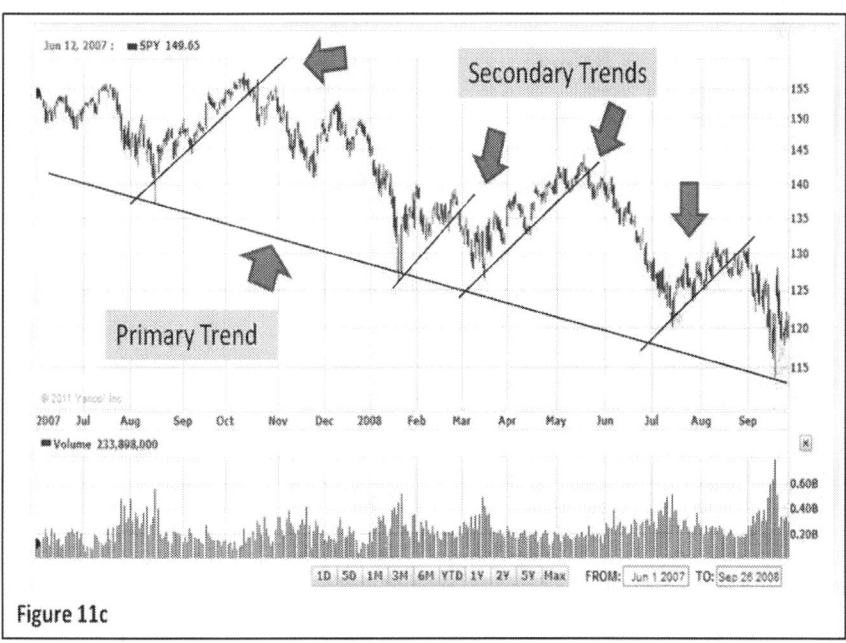

Figure 11c

Besides the obvious fact that secondary trends do also happen during a declining primary trend, the first thing you should notice is the volume. Since we will be going into more depth about trading these trends later, you should familiarize yourself with how volume confirms the primary trend.

The primary trend is down, so on the declines, the volume is higher. Although these secondary trends are actually advances, the volume during these advances is still lower, and then increases on the subsequent declines. So the higher volume is confirming the primary trend.

Let's take a close-up look at the first secondary trend on the preceding chart. It began its advance in mid-August and ended about 60 days later in mid-October where it resumed the decline with the primary trend. See Figure 11d below.

Figure 11d

First of all, notice the extremely low volume on this secondary trend, leading up to and including, the high it

Trading the Trends

made in mid-October. In comparison, it is about one-half the volume heading into the prior low. Trying to trade these bounces is very difficult. As you can imagine, a short-term trader would be forced to use the minor trends, or pullbacks, within the secondary trend to gain any insight as to sustained direction, albeit even short-term direction of the stock. By the time any significant pullback in the secondary trend occurs and appears it might hold, it's too late to enter. The trader would be late to the party, so to speak.

But traders with a higher risk tolerance, even knowing the primary trend was down, would see the low at $140 made with a positive trading day, enter quickly and place a stop loss just below the $140 mark. Yes, this is a high risk move since there is no confirmation the low would actually hold. There is obviously the chance the stock would trade higher for only a day or two and then head south again, thus, handing the trader a small loss. If a stop loss is not used then the loss might not be small at all. On the flip side of that coin, if he is right, and the stock advances as it did, then he makes a very nice $12 to $15 profit depending on when he closes the trade. About a 10% gain, but a very risky move.

That may sound easy. But in a declining market one must always keep in mind **the momentum is down**. So the chances of being right and grabbing that nice profit become very slim. So before you think about trying such a move, take a closer look at the chart and realize there are numerous days the stock pauses its decline, trades higher for only a day or two, and then heads down again. Then think which one of those you would have *picked* as a possible bottom.

©Copyright McAllen Publishing

Trading the Trends

That is a good example that the shorter the trading time frame, the easier it is to be wrong. That is also a great lesson in staying on the *right* side of the market. The primary trend is the **Granddaddy,** and until it changes direction, it certainly is wise to follow what he says. Otherwise Granddaddy will slap you back into submission.

Secondary trends within a declining primary trend are very tricky. We will go much more in depth about them later when we discuss entering and managing trades, but let's take a look at the other secondary trends shown on the previous chart (Figure 11c). There are a couple of things I should point out about them before we move on. See Figure 11e below.

Figure 11e

The first of the two secondary trends lasted about 6 weeks and the second lasted about 8 weeks. Both resulted in a bounce of about 10% from the beginning to the end of each trend.

Notice the second secondary trend did not start from the primary trend line. In fact, where it began would have been considered by technical traders as the stock making a double bottom, or retesting the lows.

Retesting the lows, or making a double bottom near the previous low is a positive sign. This is a common chart pattern indicating support has been found and then tested. The above pattern would fool some traders into thinking a low had been found and the primary trend was changing. Obviously this was the case since after the second low the stock then made a higher high. A very alluring move.

During a declining market, most traders are looking for any sign of a bottom. And when the market, or a stock, retests the lows and begins advancing, buying interest will be sparked. But remember the channel line? Let's look how easy it is to be reasonably sure if a bottom has been found.

See Figure 11f following.

Figure 11f

The above chart is the same chart we began our discussion with regarding secondary trends. I only added a channel line. You see, by connecting the very first two highs and extending the line, each time the stock entered a secondary trend it stayed within the channel.

There were times it didn't decline back to the trend line and times it didn't advance all the way up to the channel line, but stayed within the range. It is often so tempting to jump back in with hopes of making money. But this tool can help protect your capital by keeping the bigger picture in perspective. We would obviously be looking for a stock to break out of the channel before stepping in and risking our money.

Chapter 10

The Three – Five Market

Minor Trends

The third trend of the 3-trend market is the minor trend. These little movements are pretty much just 'noise' to the long-term investor. They can last from an hour or two to a week or more. Day traders thrive on them, along with their Rolaids, Mylanta, and other powerful mind-altering drugs to calm their emotions and nerves.

Instead of spending time on how nerve-wracking trying to trade or invest while using these little movements would be, let's use them as an example of the bigger picture. This will give you a much broader understanding of market movement in general. It will also give you a tool to use that will help you anticipate change before it happens.

The Three – Five Market

The market has three trends, the primary, secondary and minor. There are three phases, the accumulation, participation, and distribution. Historically the market likes three and five. It will advance for about three or five days and then pullback for three or five days before repeating this cycle again and again. These moves are what cause the stair-step advances and declines that show on the charts.

We will start with the same charts we have just used. See Figure 11d below.

Figure 11d

Starting with the first advance on the left side of the preceding chart, notice the 3-day advance and then the 5-day decline.

As you look across the chart you will notice this repeating many times. By counting the daily bars, the numbers three and five will show up repeatedly.

Many times the daily bar count may be a day or two off one way or the other, but the general moves show up many times as either three or five days. For more examples see Figure 11e below.

Figure 11e

As you look at different charts, you will notice this whether it is within the primary trend, the secondary trend, or just the minor trends.

Trading the Trends 106

The point is, many times when a stock advances and then begins a decline, it may not resume its advance for three or five days. Conversely, advances normally last three or five days.

That is just one of those tidbits of information that will be helpful at times. For instance, when considering buying a stock but the chart shows it has been in an advance for 5 consecutive days. One might want to re-think the entry point and give the stock time to pullback.

But let's look at how this carries over into the bigger picture. The market has 3 'Legs'. See Figure 12a below.

Figure 12a

©Copyright McAllen Publishing

Trading the Trends

Historically the market moves in threes. Not only are the 3-day and 5-day moves very common in the shorter time frames, the market moves in threes in the big picture as well.

Three legs up and three legs down. The preceding chart shows the primary trend leading up to the high in 2000.

See how each leg up is clearly defined and separated by a correction. These corrections are secondary trends, but they do define the overall 3-leg movement. The ensuing decline and subsequent bear market following the 2000 high was no different.

See Figure 12b below.

Figure 12b

Trading the Trends

It doesn't get much prettier than that. Once again the 3 legs are very distinct starting from the highs in 2000 and then trending down to the lows of the bear market.

Look at the following bull market's three legs leading up to the 2007 high.

See Figure 12c below.

Figure 12c

Then from the highs of 2007 to the end of the bear market in 2009, again the market took its three steps down. See Figure 12d following.

Figure 12d

Although the first step was not as noticeable on the chart, it was still more than a 20% drop from a high of nearly $160 per share down to $125. A 25% decline classifies as entering a bear market. So the very first leg landed very close to bear market territory.

Realizing the market historically trades in 3-day and 5-day moves in the minor trends and also has three legs to most every major advance and decline can be helpful. It is not something to base your trading decisions on, but can certainly be a bit of information to keep in mind when making your decisions.

For instance, look at the preceding chart at the end of the second leg down. From the bounce and volatility it's apparent that many buyers were thinking that was the bottom. The volume was high, even on some of the up-days further indicating buying interest. But the investor realizing there could be a third leg down still yet to come would be very hesitant to do any early buying.

Sure, I could speculate that the three legs to major moves are a part of the market phases and I might be right. The first leg may be the end of the accumulation phase, the second leg may be the public participation phase, and the third may be the excess phase and early distribution. Whether I'm right or not is trivial. What is important is that you realize they do happen and use that to your advantage. For instance, when the market pulled back in March 2007 and then began the final advance. See figure 12c following.

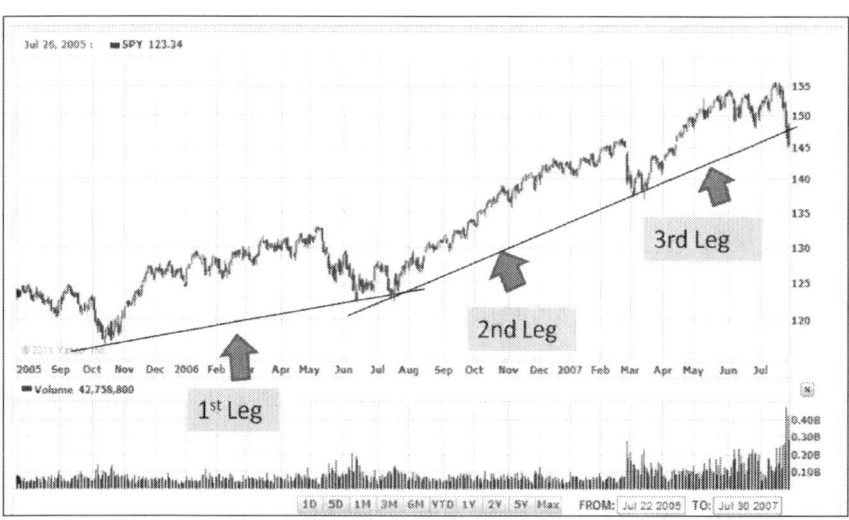

Figure 12c

Trading the Trends

If you pulled up the preceding chart as the market moved higher from the March low and saw the two legs already formed, you would likely realize the market may be entering the third leg and be looking to cut back and start moving to safety during a further advance. Thus, you would be distributing by supplying the market with your shares. Remember, as the price advance continues, the risk becomes greater.

Also, during the minor trends when you are watching for an entry point to purchase, if you notice the stock has traded down only one or two days, it might be wise to wait a day or so to make sure another down day is not ahead. As an example see Figure 11e below.

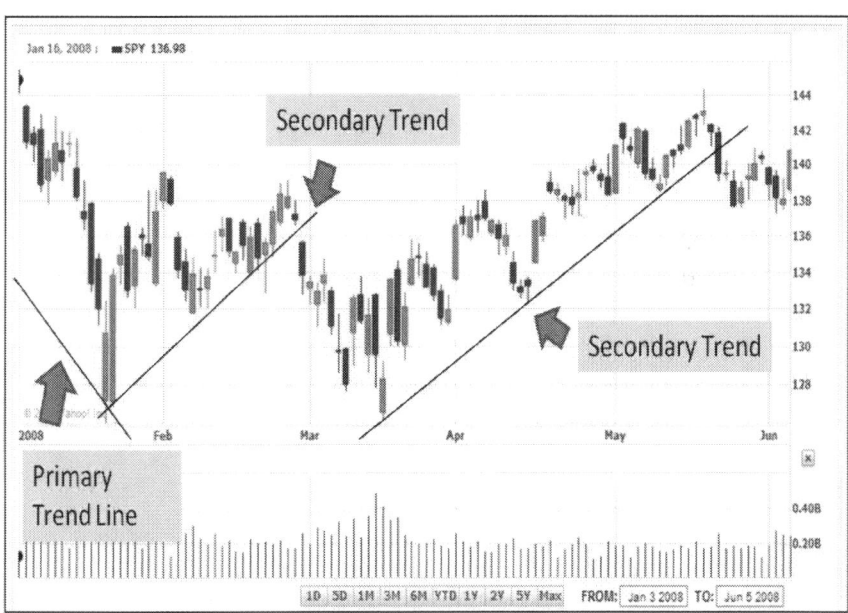

Figure 11e

Trading the Trends

Notice on the very left side the preceding chart how the stock declined and then traded higher for two days, down one day, then up one day. It then fell $10 per share over the next four days.

Needless to say, while viewing any chart you will see the three – five market in the primary trends, secondary trends and the minor trends. You will also see how the market consistently moves in three legs, both up and down. There will also be times you will see these three legs, not just in the primary trends, but also the secondary trends. Even in the preceding chart, each secondary trend has three legs. They are not quite as visible as they are on the long-term charts of a primary trend, but they are still there.

So file that bit of information away to use to your advantage from time to time whether you are looking for an entry point or an exit point. We have covered significant territory learning about the market, its trends, phases, and trading ranges.

Let's make some trades.

Now, this book is different from other books. Most books will simply show you a chart that has already formed and find some creative way to tell you *why* you should have bought at the bottom and sold at the top.

As the investor, you need to gain knowledge from the experience and thought processes of the trader as the decision is made to enter a trade. You then must learn how to manage your trade, protect your capital, and know when to exit. So we are going to go from start to finish on a number of

©Copyright McAllen Publishing

trades using the charts as they are forming. Thus, you will learn from the thought process of the trader as information is analyzed and decisions are made.

> "When share markets are booming it's easy to believe the propaganda that shares will always bounce back from a fall and that shares always outperform other investments over the long term."
> ~Annette Sampson

Chapter 11

Entering a Trade

First of all, we aren't going to invest or trade in any individual stocks because the risk is just too high. We don't want our hard-earned money going down the tubes with another Enron, MCI, or even a company that doesn't use accounting magic. Even good companies can be hit by a lawsuit, recall of products, or some other isolated event that can cause an immediate and drastic drop in share price. And we don't want that risk.

You should also be aware that companies who lead the charge during bull market runs often fall during the next bear market and never recover. For instance, companies like Microsoft, Intel, and Sun Microsystems. After making highs in 2000, Microsoft and Intel lost more than 50% of their value, and eleven years later (2011) have never recovered.

Trading the Trends

Sun Microsystems, the maker of the popular JAVA computer application and many hardware components lost 99% of its value and was finally purchased for pennies on the dollar compared to its price during the boom.

Historically, it has always been new leaders that emerged after a bear market and lead the market back up. So that is another reason we don't put all our eggs in one basket. Instead, we stick with trading and investing in the overall market. We have used SPY, the index for the S&P 500, in our examples and we will continue to stay with it.

The Big Picture

The first thing we want to know is what the overall market has done, is doing, and then use that information to reasonably determine what it is likely to do. So we start with the big picture, a 5-year chart.

Note: I have used free charts from Yahoo throughout the book so the average investor can clearly see that using paid charting services or some elaborate trading tools are not necessary to be successful *Trading the Trends*.

The following chart is a 5-year chart of SPY and I simply included the 200- and the 50-day moving averages.

See Figure 13 following.

©Copyright McAllen Publishing

Figure 13

The big picture shows the SPY reaching nearly $160 per share at the top and then the primary trend changed heading into the bear market.

The first thing you should notice is the major decline, and the three legs down in particular. We can tell by the wide trading ranges at the end of the second leg down that many thought that was the bottom. They began buying at the end of the near freefall thinking they were *picking* the bottom.

The second thing you should notice is the 200-day moving average. As the stock was trading in the up-trend toward the high in late 2007, every time it declined it found support at or near the 200-day moving average (200 DMA). This average acts as both support and resistance. As you can see in late 2007 the SPY fell below the 200 DMA and then traded back up to touch it, but did not advance above the resistance.

So when we are looking to buy, we want our stock to be advancing and be on top of the 200 DMA.

The third thing to notice is the channel line. By connecting the two highs and extending the line we see the stock is back up very close to the upper channel line around $95 per share. Granted, we could redraw the channel line using the last high at $105 before the lowest low which would show the stock already breaking out of the channel. But that would be a mistake because that would indicate a breakout from the channel before the stock ever traded above the last high. And that high will inevitably be a point of resistance during any future advance. So the only highs we have to use are the first ones entering the decline.

And no, that channel line is not pretty. Neither is the near freefall the stock experienced during the second leg down. But declines are seldom attractive. So we use what information we have available to draw a correct channel line.

Looking at this chart on June 8, 2009, we see SPY crossed back above the 200 DMA just a couple of days ago. We also see the 50 DMA that has been in decline for more than a year has turned back up. These are two good positives. So let's take a closer look.

See figure 13a below.

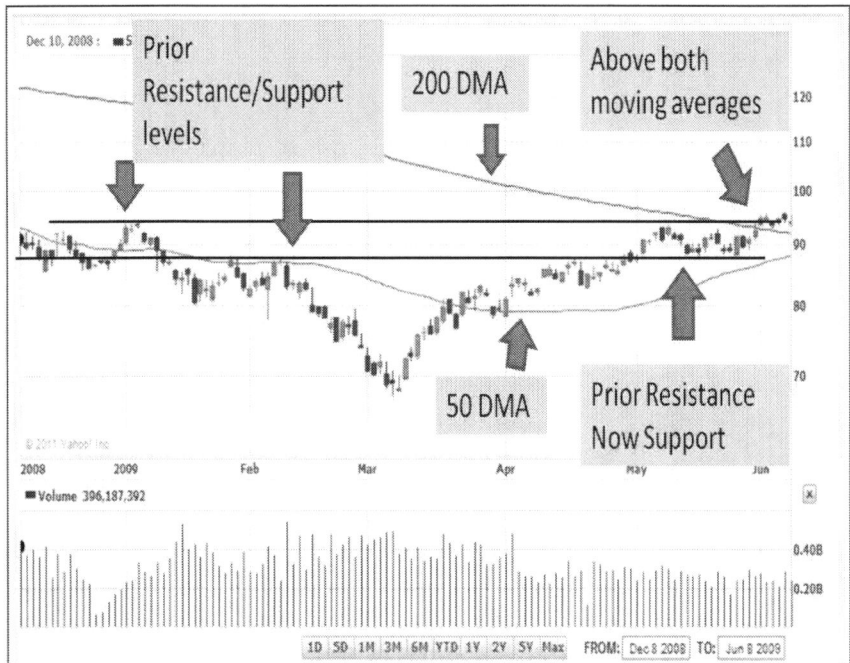

Figure 13a

The above 6-month chart gives a bit more information. Notice the support/resistance lines I included on the chart. Back in February during the bottoming process the stock tried to advance two times but couldn't trade above the $88 price. This tells us there was at least minor resistance at that level since the stock eventually declined further. But once a stock breaks through a known resistance, that prior resistance then becomes support. Looking further across the chart, we see after making the lowest low, the stock traded back to that resistance line, fell back a little, and then traded higher to cross it.

The resistance then became support as it tested it two times before finally advancing to cross above the 200 DMA.

Trading the Trends

At this point we have some positives. Let's analyze the possible setup.

1. It is above both moving averages.
2. It is above prior known resistance.
3. It is in an uptrend (possibly secondary)
4. There is support at the 200 DMA just a couple dollars below the current price.
5. There is known support at the support and resistance line at $88.
6. The 50 DMA is up-trending and currently right around $88 to $90 per share. So there would also be some minor support there as well.
7. The volume looks favorable. There seems to be slight increased volume on most up days and decreased volume on most down days.

But there are also some negatives. Mainly, there has been no significant pullback since the lowest low to draw a new trend line. The only trend line we can draw is using the lows on the minor trends, which is not that effective or reliable. Realizing there could be a significant pullback, any trade would have to have a tight stop loss just below the $88 support. Beyond that, the next level of support would be the lowest low at about $70. That is certainly too far away.

Another thing is, we can't forget our upper channel line is also sitting right on $95 per share. That may cause some resistance also. But let's take a closer look to see if we can learn something more by using a 3-month chart to get more exact. See Figure 13b following.

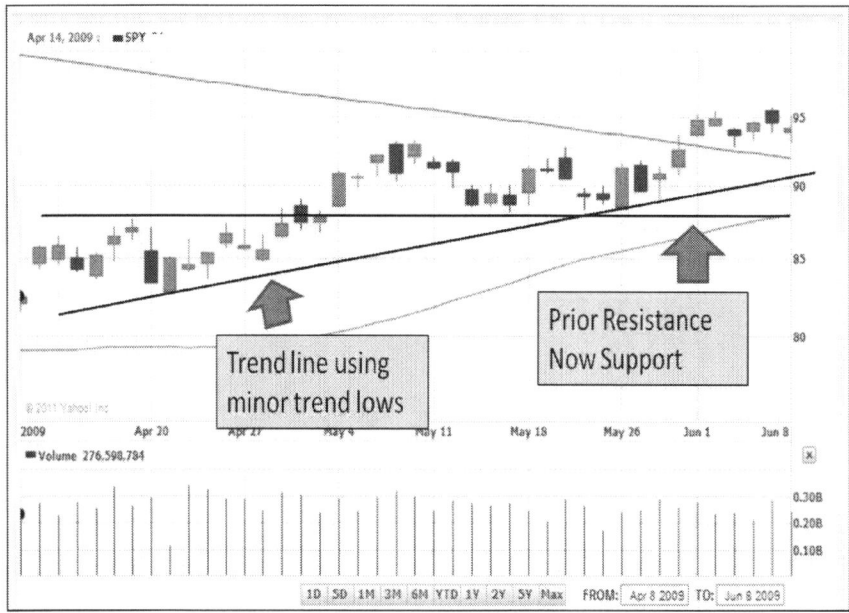

Figure 13b

In the above 3-month chart, the trend line does provide some information even though it is drawn using the minor trend lows. We can see after making the high of about $93 in the middle of the chart, there was a 5-day pullback, about a 3-day advance, another 3-day pullback and then a 5-day advance. Our trend line is above support but still below the 200 DMA.

We also see the last advance was up to $95 per share which is shown on the 6-month chart as minor resistance. The stock has since bumped its head on that and has been unable to cross it.

The bottom line is... we need to wait. Here's why:

1. Right now the stock is at about $94 per share. It's just under a known minor resistance level of $95 and likely very close to our upper channel line as well. It has no headroom to advance without first hitting resistance.

2. It has advanced for five days with no pullback. So it may be due for at least a small decline.

3. It also appears to be trading flat – bumping it's head on the resistance.

4. It is about $2 above the 200 DMA, $3 above our trend line, and $6 above reasonable support.

Possibly in a few days it might return to the trend line which will tell us if the trend line will hold, and it will also be closer to support. When we buy, we want to place a stop loss just below known support. Buying now would mean our stop loss would be more than a $6 per share loss in the event it declined and the support didn't hold. Especially since it only has roughly $1 headroom before hitting known resistance.

Although it appears to be holding its own at the current level, it would be risky to buy that far away from support. So let's give it some time to move one way or the other before we decide.

Eleven days later on June 19, we see the stock has declined; it appears to have found support on the 200 DMA for a second time but fell below our trend line. See Figure 13c below.

Figure 13c

It was unable to break through the resistance at $95 after trading there for 10 consecutive days. Now, since declining three days it has only advanced for two days. We need to wait. It is now about $5 away from $88 support level, but that support is minor and we don't know if it will hold.

It might appear we are counting pennies here. But if you take care of the pennies, the dollars will take care of themselves. We don't want to buy at $93 when we know there is resistance $2 away and support is $5 the other way.

So we need to wait so it can either return to support and test the support level or trade above the resistance and close above it.

Note: A close *above* resistance is important, especially on higher volume. That would indicate buying interest, strength and momentum. Trading above resistance during a trading day only to fall back below it to close is not significant. It must have the strength and momentum to move above it and stay. We always use the closing price as indicators from a technical perspective. There is an old saying:

"Novices open the market, but the pros close it."

There is considerable truth to that. The closing price also eliminates most of the day-trading liquidity in the market since most of those traders close all positions by the end of the day. Therefore, the closing price includes the serious buyers, usually the pros, and indicates what their interests really are, either positive or negative. At the same time, the daily fluctuations can drive a stock up or down only to return to the normal range.

What we want to see here is momentum and strength. The stock is showing strength in holding its own, but still lacks the momentum to move higher. And many times when momentum is lacking, volume will be lacking also. If a move higher is on low volume it usually will not hold.

©Copyright McAllen Publishing

On July 14, we have been watching this stock for more than a month waiting for it to present us with the opportunity to buy at a reasonably safe entry point. See Figure 13d below.

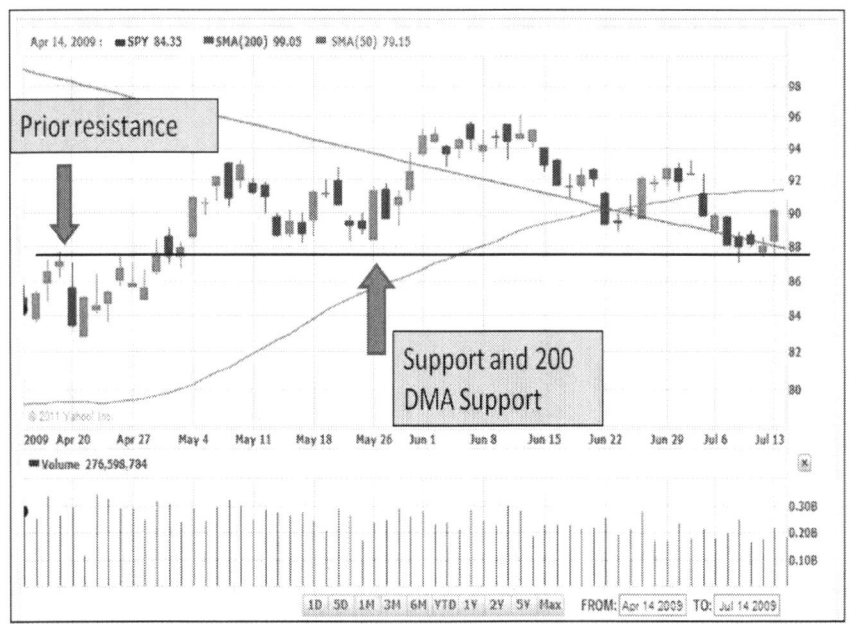

Figure 13d

Our prior trend line using the minor trends is no longer valid since it was broken about a week ago. But we do have a low risk opportunity now to buy with a possible high return. That is what we want.

Let's look at the positives.

1. The $88 support level has been tested three times and held. Possibly four times if you want to count the low in June. The big positive candle on the extreme right side of the chart shows increased volume.

Trading the Trends

2. The stock has now traded down to the 200 DMA three times and held above it. Each time either closing right on the line or very near to the line. Yesterday, July 12, it closed just below it on a positive day but close enough to it. And then today it advanced above it to close at the high of the day. Closing at the high of the day is a positive sign and also an indication it will advance further in the near term. Remember, we are looking at the closing price. There was no late-day sell-off and buying interest and momentum was positive right up to the closing bell. We know this because there is no wick extended on the top of that candle. (Remember, the wick of the candle is the daily trading range.)

3. At $90 per share, known resistance is $5 away and support is $2 lower at $88.

Buying at this point we will place our stop loss at $87.50 in the event it falls below support.

Trader thoughts: This is an early entry since we have yet to have a decisive higher low to draw a trend line that would indicate a new primary trend. Yet, we did not try to pick a bottom. We can see it has been in the bottoming process for about six months while in the accumulation phase. This is very clear on the 6-month chart. We know the stock has already advanced about $20 since the lowest low, so it is already in an uptrend and had the momentum and strength to push through a resistance level at $88, push through another resistance being the 200 DMA, and stay above the

200 DMA. It has successfully tested the support level and tested the support of the 200 DMA three times.

Yes, it might be better if the 200 DMA was also headed upward. But it takes considerable time for it to do that since it is a slow moving average based on 40 weeks of trading. According to the technical analysis, the resistance line at $95 extended straight across the 6-month chart clearly shows the bottoming process and the accumulation phase. A move above $95 would be the break-out point.

An investor who wanted to take even less risk would wait for the stock to break-out of this bottom. A break-out on strong volume above $95 would definitely remove most doubt that a new trend was beginning. So at this point, there are two schools of thought and a decision to be made. Do we wait for a break-out or do we buy close to support expecting a break-out?

If we wait for the stock to break-out above $95, and we are hoping that it does, then the break-out would definitely be a positive sign, but it would also mean we are buying further away from support. Yet, a tight stop loss could still be placed giving the stock a little breathing room but protecting our capital.

If we buy close to current $88 support and we are wrong, we stand to lose only $2.50 per share. At the same time, we have the propensity of evidence this stock truly has the ability to at least hold at this level and will most likely move higher.

That is the best we can do. In **Trading the Trends**, our goal is to only put our money at risk when the odds are in our favor. This is done by simple research, knowledge of the market, technical analysis, and letting the market come to us.

That is exactly what we did.

- We used technical analysis to find support/resistance
- We waited for a good entry point above the 200 DMA.
- We made sure the stock could hold support.
- We allowed it to return to, and test, that support.

And most importantly, we are going the limit our risk. Not only are we buying after careful planning and patience, we are going to place a stop loss under the support level. In the worst-case scenario we will only lose $2.50 per share.

Another possible scenario is the stock trades back up to the $95 resistance and fails to break-out once again. If so, we are counting on the $88 support to hold and we will still only lose $2.50 per share if it doesn't.

So based on this analysis, if we waited for it to break-out above the $95 resistance before buying, then that resistance would then be support and our stop loss would be below it. Therefore, we would be looking at virtually the same dollar amount of risk involved. It's an early trade. Because it has moved above the 200 DMA for the first time since the previous primary declining trend began, we are anticipating it has begun a new primary trend and is headed upward. So let's place the trade.

Chapter 12

> Time is your friend; impulse is your enemy.

Placing the Trade

Before placing the trade, there are three things that must be done.

1. Find or wait for an entry point
2. Know where support is for the stop loss
3. Know resistance levels and possible target

We have completed the first two things on the list, but we must know any other resistance levels that might possibly prevent a move higher. This will also give us an idea as to a possible target price.

For instance, if the stock has never been above a certain price in the past, then we would be looking for it to have trouble advancing above that price now, or in the future. History does repeat itself. And as we have seen by using

Trading the Trends

technical analysis, prior support and resistance is a very powerful investing and trading tool.

To find other possible resistance, we look at a 1-year chart in order to see where the stock has traded in the past. From this we can get a very good idea as to the level it may trade to, or have trouble trading above. See Figure 13e below.

Figure 13e

The above chart includes our $95 resistance level, and I also included a new trend line using the current lows. We don't know if the current low will hold, but we are inclined to believe it will given the fact the stock has held this low three times. This is a very interesting setup. The new trend line and the resistance line create an ascending triangle. The 200 DMA and new trend line create a symmetrical triangle. The new trend line and our channel line (not shown) would create another symmetrical triangle.

In my book, **'Charting and Technical Analysis,'** I describe these triangles forming in chart patterns as a wedge, but I'll give you a short lesson here as well. As these forces converge, something has to give. Either the stock has to break down below our trend line, or has to advance above the resistance.

Since our trend line is right on the 200 DMA, if it breaks down, it would also have to break below the 200 DMA, which it has not done in the last three attempts. This wedge is like squeezing a juice box. As pressure is applied, something has to give. End of that lesson; let's get back to finding possible resistance for our stock.

We see there might be some minor resistance at the $100 level. During the decline heading to the bottom, a rally took it back to $100 before it turned and headed down again. It did trade back up to that level three times within about 30 days before dropping to a major low (the second leg down). That is a 'round' number ($100), and historically those are often psychological resistance. But prior to that, the next resistance would be up around $130. So, in the event the stock advances as we expect, we should expect the known resistance at $95 and at least some resistance at $100.

Make the Trade

Depending on your risk tolerance level, you must decide how much money you are going to risk. Since support is at $88, we want our stop loss just under that level at about $87.50, so our maximum loss is $2.50 per share. Obviously that translates into $2500 for 1000 shares if the stock declines. But just to keep our numbers for losses and gains easy, let's buy 1000 shares at $90 for a total of $90,000. **Done**... We are now the proud owners of SPY stock with our $90,000 investment.

DON'T MOVE!

Yes, I screamed that! Once you place your trade, **do not leave your computer without placing your stop loss!**

Stop Losses

Let's take a little time to discuss stop losses. The stop loss is one of the most important parts of your trade. Never trade without it, and never invest without it. It ranks up there in the level of importance with analysis of the general market, the primary trend, and finding a good entry point.

It is your insurance against major loss. It is how you protect your capital. It is how you limit your risk. In the event you are trading or investing in a security that your brokerage firm does not offer stop loss protection, then set an alert. If your investment falls below that level, get out. Remember this saying:

"**When in doubt – Get out.**"

Your money is much safer in your account while you are sitting on the sidelines waiting for the right opportunity than it is holding an investment that is going against you.

Never forget:

- A 50% loss in a stock or mutual fund(s) requires a 100% gain just to break even.

- A 75% loss requires a 300% gain just to break even.

Most people never recover from this type of loss. Let's put it in perspective.

If you look back at the 2-year chart on our SPY stock, it was trading at $150 per share in 2007 and early 2008. The buy-and-hold investors who purchased at that level were down more than 50% at the lowest low.

The math is easy, if they bought 1000 shares at $150 per share, or $150,000, they would have been down to less than $70,000 at one point. How many years will they hold the loss hoping to just break even? That's insane.

So use your stop loss. If you have to set an alert, when the stock reaches your alert, get out. It never means you are a bad investor or trader. It only means you may have entered at the wrong time or the market just went against you.

So sit on your money, reassess your decision, and wait for another opportunity.

Don't get creative

Some investors and traders make the mistake of trying to limit their loss with a creative stop loss such as a *Stop Limit.* Don't do it.

A stop limit is an order for your broker to sell your stock if it trades down to a certain price. But the sell order will not be executed unless a specified price is obtained.

For instance, our 1000 shares of SPY have a stop loss of $87.50. It is set *Good-till-canceled*, to sell at *Market Price* if it declines to $87.50. It's very simple and straightforward.

But if we used a Stop Limit order, we might set the *Stop* at $87.50 which would trigger the sale, but we might set the limit at $87.00. This would mean once the stock declined to $87.50 it would then only be sold at a price of $87 or higher. In a perfect world and under good market conditions this might work fine. But if the stock drops below our limit before it is sold, then we still own it and are losing. Not a good situation to be in.

If we are wrong and it declines, we would much rather have $86.90 per share or $86.20 than to still be holding when the price drops much further. So don't get creative... Just use a simple stop loss.

With our stop loss set, we are now protected in the event of a decline. In a worst-case scenario and the stock declines, we will have about $87,500 of our $90,000 investment capital left. Less than 3% of our capital was lost.

Holding losses to a minimum is vital. Many books will tell you to limit your losses to about 8%. But I see that as too much for a couple of reasons.

1. If you enter a trade or investment and it declines by 8%, the chance of it declining further becomes much greater. So you either entered at the wrong time or the stock was very weak. True, some individual stocks have a broad trading range and may drop 6% or 8% in one decline and advance more than that on the next bounce. But trading an index like the SPY, QQQ, or DIA, if they drop 8% there is something definitely wrong.

2. If you lose 8% on three trades, that is 24% of your investment dollars. That is too much.

An 8% loss on this trade would be $7200. That is why we always buy close to support. We would have to be wrong three consecutive times to lose that much money.

And I look at it this way…If a trader is wrong three times in a row then he/she is definitely missing something. Most likely, the trader obviously is either trading against the trend, buying tops, or has grossly missed what the market is saying.

About the only other possibility would be the market might be in a very volatile stage. And if that's the case, you have no business trying to trade. That's when you either observe or go fishing. You cannot fight the market. It will always win and you will always lose. Period. End of story. So if losing becomes frequent, then shut up and listen. The market is speaking and you are not paying attention.

Chapter 13

Managing the Trade

The great thing about **Trading the Trends** is we don't really have to watch the minute-by-minute trading of our stock. We used time-tested tools to find an entry point, and only entered the trade when the odds of success were in our favor. If we are wrong, and entered at the wrong time, then our stop loss will end the trade for us and we can go back to the drawing board, so to speak... Watching, analyzing, and waiting for another low-risk opportunity.

This is not to say that most of us won't keep a very close eye on the stock, because we just will. We want to know if we were right in our decision. Plus, we really don't want to lose 3% of our money. So the fear of being wrong and losing will definitely capture the interest of most investors and traders.

But still, we must remove the emotion. We made an informed decision based on technical analysis and time-tested techniques. If you let emotions into the fray, you will make bad decisions and lose. It's as simple as that.

Trading the Trends

This is not an emotional experience. It is logical, rational, and reasonable. So *what* if we are wrong and the stock turns and heads back down to retest the lowest low. We will not be a part of that $20 decline! Our stop loss will take us out with a small loss.

We would then have the opportunity to buy at even a lower price with even a higher possible return. That is, in the event the opportunity presented itself.

Let's check on our trade. See Figure 13f below.

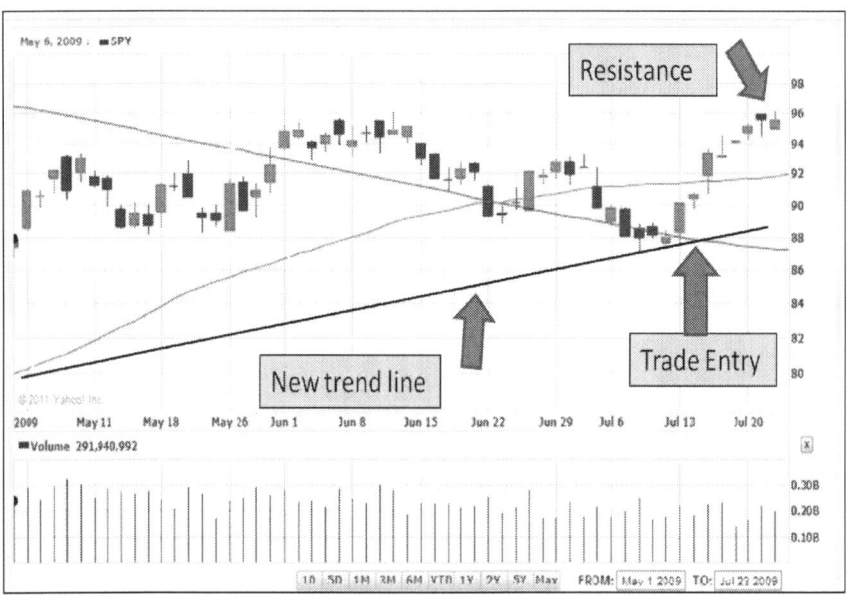

Figure 13f

The above chart shows our stock has in fact moved higher, but is once again bumping its head on the $95 resistance. After six or seven positive trading days advancing, the first negative trading day was at the resistance level.

Trading the Trends

Note: This is how powerful support and resistance levels are. Using technical analysis is the only way to recognize these market indicators. It is no accident the stock traded negative on the day it reached resistance. By looking back at the 6-month or 1-year chart, that resistance was valid then and continues to be valid.

Now, with this advance we have about a $5 per share gain. A short-term trader might jump ship and put his/her five-grand profit in the bank and wait for another pullback to buy again.

Although that is certainly one alternative, let's think it through.

More Decisions:

Watching a gain turn into a loss is never an enjoyable experience. We all seem to have the tendency to kick ourselves when we make a mistake. For instance, if this stock began a decline, watching a $5000 profit get sold out at $87.50 for a $2500 loss would be a hard pill to swallow. But at the same time, this reminds me of what an old stock speculator once said when asked if he was going to sell for a small profit.

"Then I'd lose my position."

This is true. By selling for a $5 profit we would then have to wait for another opportunity. If the stock declined back to our support, that might be another opportunity, but if it continued to advance, then where would we buy it back? We would have lost our position. We are not "holding out for top dollar"

©Copyright McAllen Publishing

because we anticipate this is simply an early entry in a new upward trend.

For the long-term investor, the best position is the one we currently have. The stock is above both moving averages, above our trend line, and has had 7 positive trading days without any pullback. Remembering the three – five market, trading more than five days in an advance with no negative trading days is a positive. So in the event there is a pullback, we might only see a 3-day decline.

Also remember the trends. A pullback or a bounce usually is 30% to 50% retracement of the previous move. Using those numbers, after a $5 advance we should expect no more than a $2.50 decline. Thus, we would still be holding a profitable position.

Another alternative is a trailing stop loss.

Trailing Stop Loss

A trailing stop loss is a stop-loss order set at a percentage level below the market price. The trailing stop price is automatically adjusted as the price fluctuates. This is such a useful tool. Using a trailing stop allows you to let profits run while cutting losses at the same time.

For instance, a trailing stop loss could now be put on our SPY stock at say, $2.50. This would protect part of the gain in the event of a decline while allowing some room for the stock to trade and move higher.

In this particular trade, it might not be a bad idea to either move our current stop loss up a little, or implement a trailing stop loss.

The reasoning is fairly simple. If the stock declines the average 30% to 50% retracement, it should not decline more than $2.50 per share. If it declined more than that, that would definitely be a sign of weakness since it would be more than the normal retracement. In all likelihood, a decline of more than 50% of this advance would see the stock head back down to retest the $88 support level.

Thus, there might be a buying opportunity if that happened, and there is no reason to lose 3% of the investment when we would likely be able to buy again at support.

So we are moving our stop loss up to $92. That gives our stock more than enough room for a 50% retracement and guarantees us a $2-per-share profit. If it declines, then we will sit on our money and wait for another opportunity.

We would rather draw minimal interest on our money than watch it evaporate in a declining investment. As we keep a close eye on our stock, let's see how it did at the resistance level.

See Figure 13g following.

Trading the Trends 140

Figure 13g

On August 7, with the stock now trading at $100 per share, we have a good profit, and about a 10% return on our investment. We certainly don't want to lose this gain so we need to analyze our trade.

I must say again how powerful and accurate support and resistance are as predictors. Our stock traded two days at the $95 resistance level before breaking through it. Notice the breakout on strong volume. This is definitely a positive. This prior resistance is now support. So we are moving our stop loss up to $94.50, just below the new support level.

Further analyzing the progress, we see it has found the resistance at $100 just as we suspected. It has traded about four days there and the last two days have been negative, closing down each day.

©Copyright McAllen Publishing

There is another lesson to be learned here. Particularly, why we can't raise our stop loss to be just below the current price.

Notice the gaps in trading at about $98, four days and six days (candles) before the end of our chart. Gaps in trading are created when a stock opens for trading either higher or lower than it closed the previous day. In this case, these are upside gaps since the stock opened higher than the previous day close. This offset in price shows up on the chart as a gap between the candles.

Historically, the market does not like gaps. And more times than not, they are closed. Meaning, sometime in the future, normally within days, the stock will either decline, or advance if the gap is created during a decline, and close the gap. The last gap is not too significant because the wick of the candles appear to have closed it. The candle wick is the trading range for the day and that one appears to have been closed during those trading days. But the other gap at $98, six days from the end of the chart is certainly open.

In our situation, the stock would have to trade back down to $98 to close that gap. Therefore, it would be risky to place a stop loss higher since during a trading day the stock could trade low enough to close that gap and take us out. Therefore we are keeping our stop loss at $94.50, just below the $95 level that previously was resistance and now will be support. This will still protect much of our gain in the event of a significant decline.

©Copyright McAllen Publishing

Trading the Trends | 142

This trade has been a success; but let's look at its next move and analyze further.

See Figure 13h below.

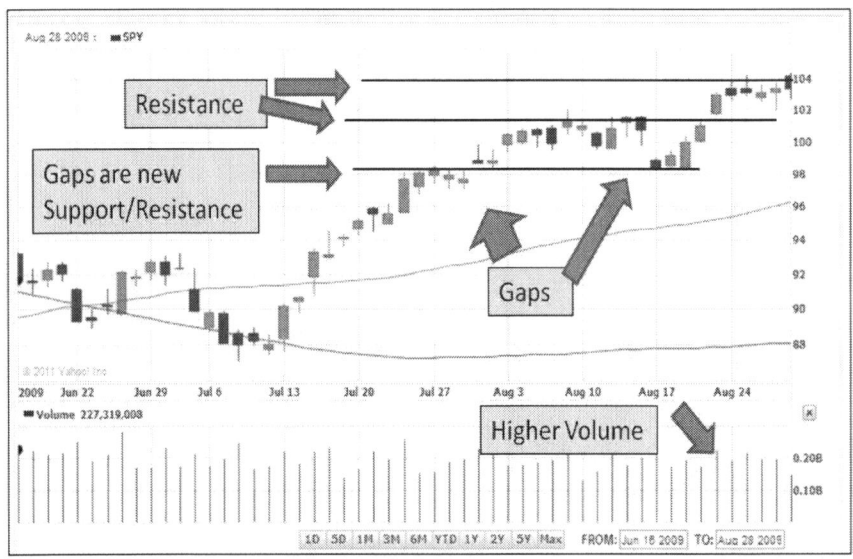

Figure 13h

On August 20, we see the stock has broken out above the $100 resistance level and has now found new resistance at $104. But there is much to learn from this chart, and as a Trend Trader, this a great learning experience.

Remember the gap at $98? We see on August 17 the stock traded down to close that gap. Yet another gap was created on the decline and closed on the ensuing advance. But another gap was created at $101 on the next move higher when the stock broke out above the $100 resistance. So we should also anticipate that one being closed as well.

©Copyright McAllen Publishing

More about Gaps

Once a gap is created it can act as support and resistance. This is clearly shown at the $98 level. The gap was closed by the stock trading back down to that level, but the gap also acted as support and the stock traded for three days without breaking the support of the gap and then traded higher from that point.

This is not a coincidence. It is something that happens quite often. Although gaps are often closed, a stock that is experiencing numerous gaps during an advance is a sign of strength and healthy buying interest.

You see, in order for the stock to create a gap, there usually must be some event to cause the increase in price prior to the market opening for trading. Maybe a company announced a new product, better than expected earnings, etc.

Our stock is the SPY which is an index of the 500 largest companies, and makes a very diversified stock portfolio. So there was likely not an earnings announcement that caused a gap in this security.

More than likely there was news related to the overall economy that created more buying interest in stocks. We may never know the reason for a gap, the reason is not necessarily important. We just need to recognize their potential from a technical perspective. As we clearly see, they are effective for support.

Since the old gap at $98 was closed and the resistance at $100 has been broken, we are anticipating the new gap being eventually closed. So our stop loss can now be raised to just below those support levels and the new gap that was created at $101. So we will raise our stop loss to $99.50.

With our stop loss at this level we are now guaranteed a 10% return on our investment. Our stock is advancing nicely, but not all roads lead to Oz. There has been no significant pullback and at this point all we have are the minor trends. So we have been using technical analysis to protect our gain and let our profit run.

You can see from the previous chart that placing a stop loss, or trailing stop loss, too close to the current price could get you taken out of the trade. Many traders make this mistake.

For instance, once our stock broke above the $95 resistance and moved up to $101 to $102, it would have been tempting, and a mistake, to move the stop loss up or only have a $2.50 trailing stop loss. Closing the gap at $98 would have hit a tight stop loss and taken us out.

The next chart shows the gap at $101 was closed with a decline back to $100.

See Figure 13i below.

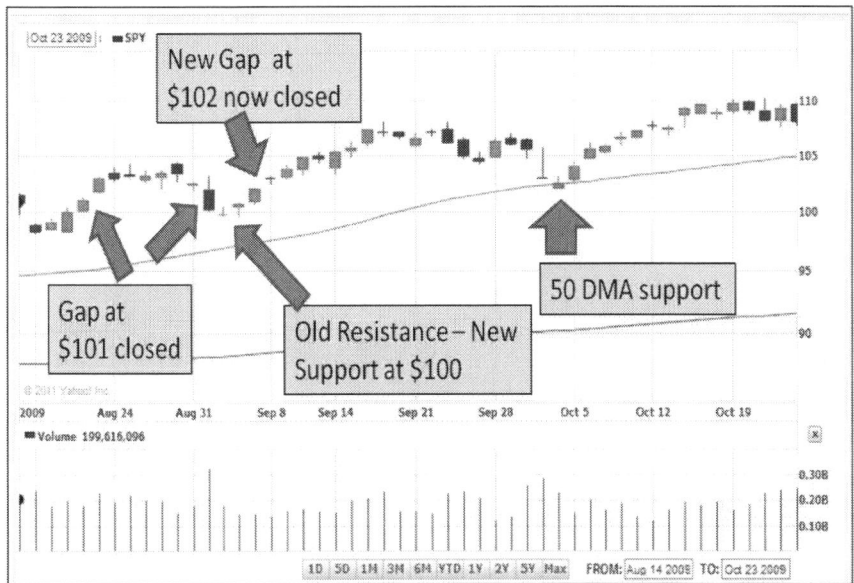

Figure 13i

Another gap was created at $102 on the move up to $107 but was closed on the next decline. You should notice the moving averages. Both the 50 and the 200 DMA are now in an uptrend. This is ideal for a healthy advance. Also notice how the 50 DMA acted as support. Historically, the 50 DMA will act as minor support. The 200 DMA is significantly more powerful as support, but at this time it has only had time to begin its turn upward and is too far from our stock to be used for anything other than an indicator that the overall market is definitely in an uptrend.

As you have noticed, we have not drawn a new trend line since there has been no significant low to use as the second low required for drawing one.

Trading the Trends 146

But when **Trading the Trends** we must keep our eye on the big picture. So let's look at what we have. See Figure 13j below.

Figure 13j

The above chart shows a trend line using the lowest low and the only significant decline, which was our entry point. This trend line may be incorrect since it would mean the trend was broken at our current price. But we know once a primary trend is established, it continues until significant evidence proves it has changed. And currently, there has been nothing but a healthy advance and nothing to indicate a change of trend. To explain, there are two things that skew the accuracy of our trend line in the above chart.

Trading the Trends

1. Remember the accumulation phase. And at the end of an accumulation phase once the public realizes the experienced investors have been buying and a bottom is likely in place, then a rapid advance usually happens. That is what happened after the lowest low.

2. The rapid advance from the lowest low was much more than a 45 degree angle. It was almost vertical. This is not always the case, but we must use what we have since there are never any perfect cases.

Currently, we continue to only have the minor pullbacks as our trend and use technical analysis to protect our profit and our capital.

See Figure 13k below.

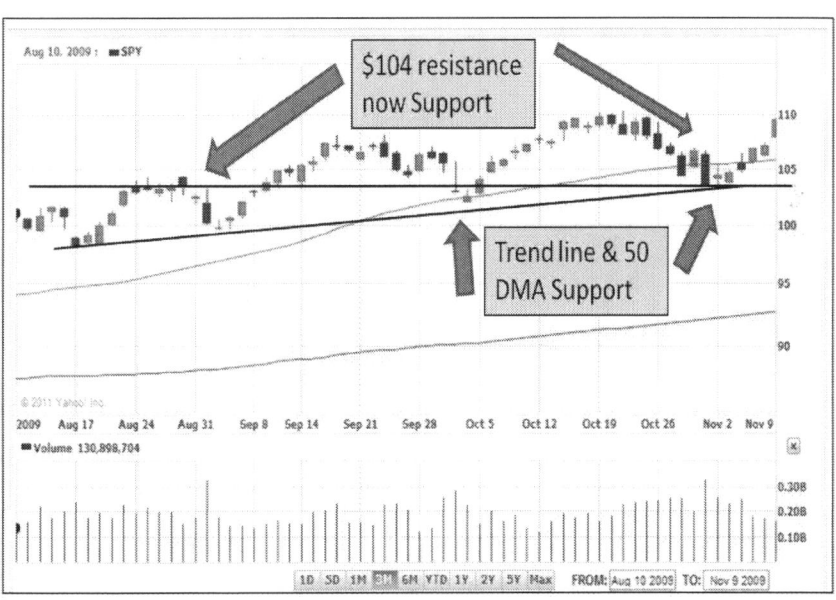

Figure 13k

It's time to check our stop loss. The gap at $102 has been closed; the stock has broken above the resistance at $104, that prior resistance is now support and has been tested. With this, it should be safe to move our stop loss up to $103.50, just below the last known support.

Notice how the trend continues while the trend line and the 50 DMA provide support. Also note the 200 DMA is now running parallel with the trend line. This is another positive.

The only negative is the stock is considerably higher than the 200 DMA. This scenario is unavoidable during the early stages of a new primary trend since the 200 DMA is a slow moving trend. However, at some point in time all stocks return to the 200 DMA. Sure, they may trade away from it for months at a time, but eventually they meet again so the Trend Trader must always keep that in mind.

But currently we have a nice profit and our stop loss will prevent losing our gain. We just have to let our stock trade. I should point out that not allowing a stock to trade is the classic mistake of many short-term traders. By placing a $2 trailing stop loss on the stock, we would have been taken out of the trade many times by now. And once we are taken out, and yes, it will happen, we then have to find another entry point.

By allowing trading room for the stock we eliminate the risk of losing our position and at the same time we are protecting most of our gains, and always protecting our capital against a major decline.

Trading the Trends   149

Let's check on our Stock.

See Figure 13l below.

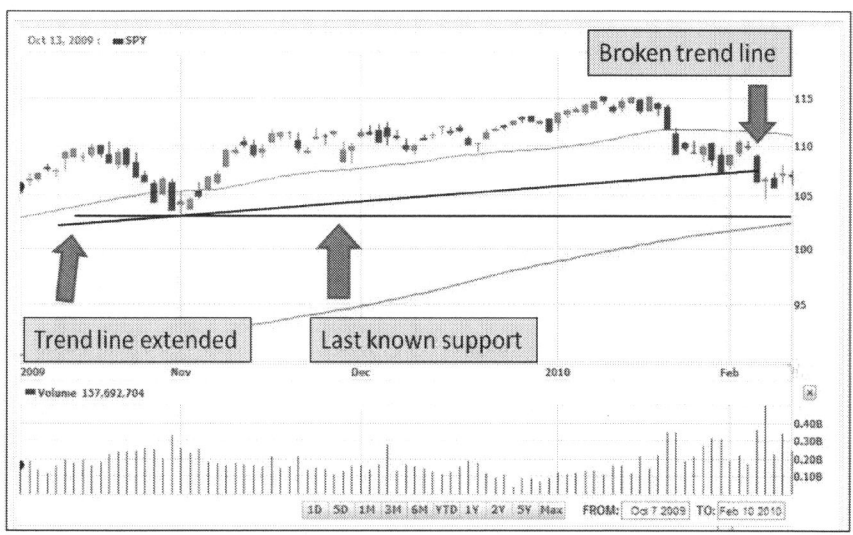

Figure 13l

We last moved our stop loss after the support at $104 was tested. Since then, the stock has entered a period of advance with relatively no pullbacks.

When the stock makes a move as shown in the above chart it will certainly get your attention. Problem is, most allow greed to adversely affect their decisions. The thought that our stock traded as high as $115 per share and we didn't jump ship is disconcerting to some. Then when the stock broke the trend line there would be added discontent.

But **Trading the Trends** is not about trying to catch every little move and then hope you are right when finding another entry point. A Trend Trader is methodical.

©Copyright McAllen Publishing

We use the information that is available to us at the time and make a logical, informed decision. Sure, it might have been great to sell out at $114, stick $24 profit ($24,000) in the bank and go fishing. And for some, that might be their decision. There are at least two schools of thought, so let's examine it closer from a technical perspective.

First of all, our stop loss is still just below the last known support. The stock has now traded down close to that support, but not broken it. It has also traded back close to the 200 DMA which is the Great-Granddaddy of all trends, but is still above it.

It has broken our trend line, but we already knew that trend line was based on the anticipation that we were entering a trade early in the trend since it was drawn using the minor pullbacks. We will be able to adjust our primary trend line when the stock establishes a definite secondary declining trend, unless our stop loss takes us out of the trade.

On the flip-side of the coin let's include a channel line and see how short-term traders may have traded.

See Figure 13m following.

Trading the Trends   151

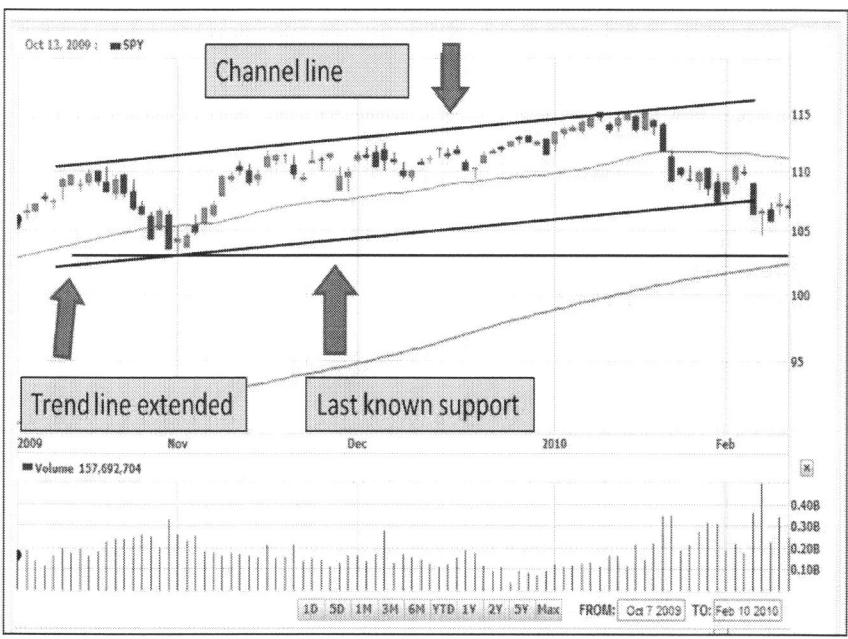

Figure 13m

During this steady up-trend the stock has consistently traded within the channel. The short-term trader would be selling every time the stock reached the top of the channel and re-entering at the bottom. This would have worked marvelously until the last decline. At that time, entering at $109 with a tight stop loss after the low would likely have caused a small loss.

For some short-term trend traders, a small loss is insignificant and expected occasionally, especially compared to the significant gains from numerous trades preceding the loss. How you decide to trade or invest is your personal decision. My goal is to give you the necessary tools.

©Copyright McAllen Publishing

The technical aspects of this pullback near $105 create considerable information. Let's look at how this changed our view from using minor trends to a much larger picture.

See Figure 13n below.

Figure 13n

The decline lasted about 30 days making it a significant secondary trend. There was a $27 advance from the previous secondary trend that ended at $88, just prior to where we entered. The $27 advance with a $10 pullback gives us a 37% correction. This is within the normal range of healthy corrections. However, it does also give us a new significant low to draw a new trend line.

The stock has also moved above the high reached before the correction. That also gives us a new support level. See Figure 13o below.

Figure 13o

From a technical analysis perspective a high preceding a significant decline is also considered significant resistance. Our stock has now traded above that resistance, tested it with one minor pullback, and continued its advance. It is time to raise our stop loss to protect more of our profit.

By placing our stop loss at $114, just below the new support level, we are also very close to our extended trend line which also indicates where the stock should find support during a normal correction. At $114 we are now guaranteed $24 profit, which is more than a 25% return on our investment.

Chapter 14

Sold Out

Protecting the profit and the capital should always be the major goal of every investor, even the longest of the long-term investors. If you have no capital, you'll never have a profit. Let's look at how our protection has paid off. Also notice the volume.

What was a healthy advance quickly became a sudden decline. Our stop loss took us out of the trade at $114. The short term traders with a tight stop loss were likely out of the trade at $118 to $120.

See Figure 13p following.

Trading the Trends

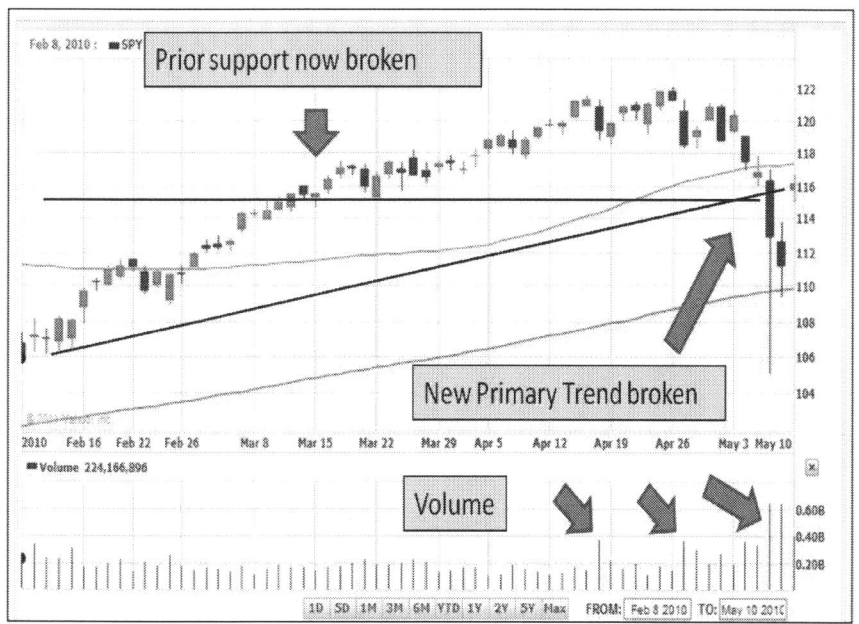

Figure 13p

So regardless of your trading preference, you should be sold out, your money in the account, and sitting on the sidelines. Our $90,000 investment lasted ten months, has grown to $114,000, is now drawing a little interest, and free of risk.

There is much to learn about the above chart, but let's start with the volume.

As we discussed early on, the volume must confirm the trend. Notice the high volume days are the down days. Not a good sign. The prior support was broken, the trend line was broken, and the 50 DMA was broken, all on higher volume. Notice the Great-Granddaddy of moving averages and the support it provides. The first day the price crossed the 200 DMA the stock had a $10 trading range on that particular day. Yet, it still closed above the 200 DMA. The second day it traded down to the 200 DMA and then closed above it.

Some long-term investors use the 200 DMA as a trigger to buy and sell because of its accuracy in support, resistance, and trends. When the market moves above the 200 DMA, they buy, and when it moves below the 200 DMA, they sell. Very simple, and most of the time is a very successful strategy.

The sideways markets are their only problem. In a sideways trending market the stock may move back and forth across the 200 DMA several times. Thus, causing several buy and sell signals, all for a small loss.

Back to the Drawing Board

Once we are sold out, it's back to the drawing board. It's time to watch, wait, and analyze. We don't get in a hurry. We will wait for a low-risk opportunity when the odds of success are heavily in our favor and protect our capital at all times.

Let's take a look at what we missed by being *stopped out* of the last trade. As it turns out, we were able to take a summer vacation. After being stopped out in May, our stock has been most uneventful for three months.

However, there are some technical analysis lessons to be learned here. First off, there have been really no significant lows to suggest the primary trend has changed.

Secondly, once the stock fell below the 200 DMA, that average then became resistance. In the following chart the stock has hit its head on the 200 DMA three times, briefly crossed it once, but is clearly seeing the resistance. See Figure 16 below.

Figure 16

Remember our $105 support level last November? It's back. After trading down to the $102 level, the stock has advanced back above the $105 support and has held for a third time. Also interesting is the resistance level around $113 to $114 which was also our stop loss level. That is not a coincidence. Support and resistance levels continue to affect the price movements for long periods of time. The $113 to $114 level was support and we had our stop loss just under it. So that old support is now resistance.

Given this sideways movement for three months and the stock below the 200 DMA, there is really no low-risk opportunity. We would certainly never buy knowing there was resistance of the 200 DMA sitting on its head.

Also notice the sideways trend and the crossing of the 200 DMA a couple of times. For long-term investors who use the 200 DMA as a buy/sell signal, that is a case where they would get several signals and none of them very good. A sideways trading range can cause them several losses and no gains.

We want to see our stock back above the 200 DMA and somewhere very close to support before we consider another purchase.

Time to Buy

After wallowing around for several months, dropping back to near $100, and banging it's head on the 200 DMA numerous times, a break-out has finally occurred.

After months of watching, we finally have another low risk opportunity. Our stock has broken above the $113 resistance level, traded on top of that old resistance for 11 days, closing below it only one time, and now advanced on higher volume. While forming this bottom, the lowest low was at $102 (shown on the previous chart), and then made a higher low at $105, which is also the old support level.

See Figure 16a following.

Figure 16a

Since we are talking technical analysis, notice the gap preceding the low and the gap *up* after the low. The two gaps at a low, one on the decline and the other on the ensuing advance creates what is called an *island reversal*. Historically this is a very powerful chart pattern indicating a move higher. Unlike normal gaps, gaps on an island reversal are seldom filled. Yet we still wanted to make sure the stock could move above the 200 DMA resistance, which it has now done.

Before we jump in, let's look at the bigger picture. It is always more telling and more accurate.

Remember; when drawing a trend line it is always best to use the most significant lows. So we have redrawn our line using the lowest lows. See Figure 16b below.

Figure 16b

By using the lowest lows, it lines up almost perfectly with the two most recent lows. Once again, that is how accurate trend lines are. The current decline is much more significant because it took two months to develop, thus, it is much more powerful. Also notice the stock is now back above both the 50 and the 200 DMA, which is where we want to see it as a buying opportunity.

I have also included a channel line connecting the highs. This will help us see any signs of early weakness in the event our stock advances as we suspect. Also included is the line indicating the next known resistance is at the $122 level.

Making the Trade

Our purchase is a low-risk opportunity with a possible high return. We have let our money sit safely on the sidelines while the direction of the market and our stock was uncertain. We have followed our strict trading and investing rules in deciding to put our money at risk.

1. We used technical analysis to find support and resistance levels
2. The stock is advancing
3. It has moved above two resistance levels, one at $113 and the other being the 200 DMA. It has tested them and held
4. It is close to support, so the stop loss can be only a few dollars away giving us minimum risk
5. Closest resistance is minor at $122

To keep the numbers easy, once more we are buying 1000 shares at $116 per share. There is known support at $114 so we will place the stop loss just below that level at $113.50. Once again we are only risking $2.50 per share with only minor resistance $6 away. So we are close to support and away from resistance.

Done!
We are the proud owners of 1000 shares of SPY. The trade is confirmed, now we place our stop loss. Again, always do this before you ever leave the computer. The stop loss *is* part of the trade, every trade.

Trading thoughts:

Some might think it's a bit silly to sell a stock at $114 only to buy it back at a higher price 4 months later. The problem with that thinking is the market doesn't always go up. In hindsight, which is always 20/20, if we had just held on to our original purchase we would have been just fine. Well, that is only true in hindsight.

At the time, when we were stopped out of the last trade there was no way of knowing if the stock would drop only another dollar or two, or if it would head back down to the lowest low of about $70 taking our $24,000 profit and handing us a $20,000 loss. The investors who held through the last two bear markets for a 50% loss wish they'd been stopped out early.

That is not a risk worth taking. Our money was safe in the account while the stock, and the market, decided on a direction it was going to take. We are currently trading in an up-trending market, and trading with the primary trend. Using the most significant lows, we have now established the parameters of the primary trend and this will help us make good decisions in the future. We followed our plan, found a good entry point very close to support, and if we are wrong we will only lose $2.50 per share.

True, this primary trend may end today, in two days, two weeks, or may resume and continue for months. We don't

Trading the Trends

know how long it will last or if we will make a profit. But our capital will be protected regardless.

We do know this: Assuming the most recent lows continue to hold, we now have definite major lows that were formed by secondary trends to draw our trend line. So when this trend line is broken it will likely be a significant reversal.

Managing the trade

Trading the Trend is not emotional. We made an informed decision using technical analysis based on time-tested techniques. We don't have to watch the ticker on TV or refresh our computer screen every few seconds to see if we are profitable. But, we probably will!

Let's see how our trade is going. After our purchase the stock traded sideways for a few days before jumping up to resistance at $122. This is the second time it has hit $122 resistance, once back in April, and now has pushed through it. Notice the volume increase as it traded up through the resistance, advanced above $122, and then made a higher minor low.

Since this resistance has been tested two times and has now become support, we will move our stop loss up to $121.50. This guarantees us a profit while keeping our stop loss just below the known resistance that is now support. See Figure 16c below.

Trading the Trends 164

Figure 16c

After about 8 months, leaving our stop loss at $121.50 using the only known support of $122, we are seeing some definite signs of weakness.

There has been a consistent advance, yet there has been one significant pullback to the $125 area. Fortunately it was not severe enough to take us out of our position. However, the primary trend line has been broken and the stock has fallen below the 50 DMA.

The 200 DMA has provided support, our stock is now trading higher, but still below the trend line. See Figure 16d below.

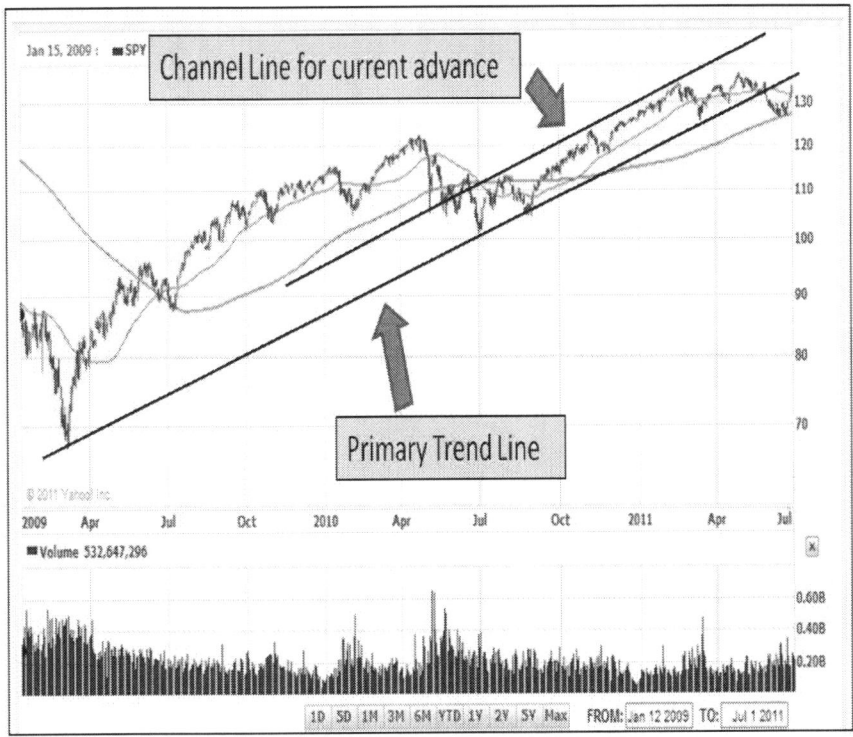

Figure 16d

Being a primary trend, this is very disheartening and is cause for concern. We also see the last two highs the stock made did not reach the upper channel, even though the channel only includes highs of the current advance. This is another sign of weakness.

It obviously does not have the strength to move higher to reach the channel line. It did so two times since our purchase, but since has failed to move back up.

Let's take a closer look. See Figure 16e below.

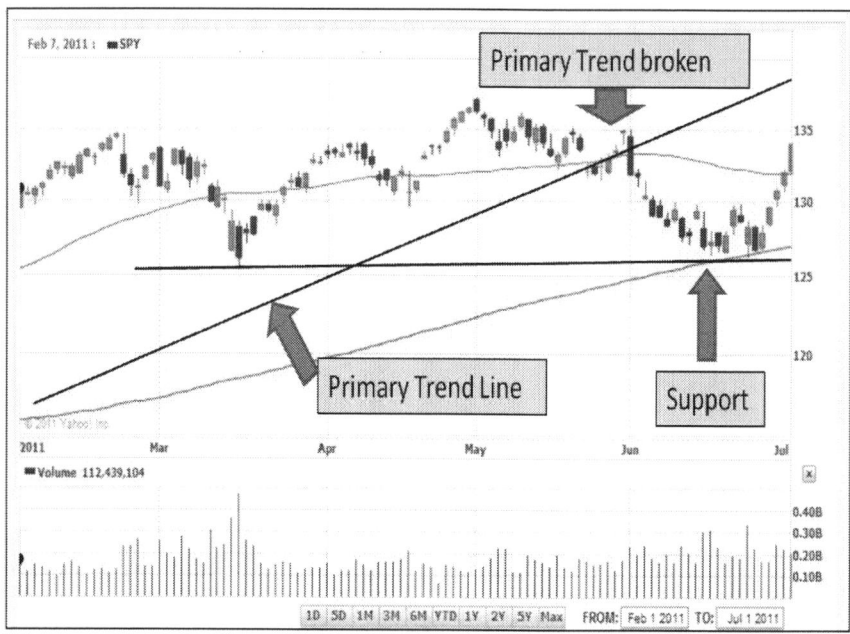

Figure 16e

This is certainly showing classic signs of weakness. First of all, look closely at the volume. Remember, it must confirm the trend.

Yet in February 2011 leading up to the first high on this chart the volume was very low and the ensuing decline saw much stronger volume.

The decline starting in May shows higher volume than the advance leading up to that high. The volume looks pretty good on the current advance off of the support of the 200 DMA but probably not as high as the volume on most of the decline down to the 200 DMA.

At this point we do not know if this is just a pullback because it is the vacation season or something more significant. At the same time we want to let our stock trade as long as we can without losing profit.

So, we now have known support at $126 per share that has been tested and the support of the 200 DMA at that same level. So we are going to move our stop loss up to $125 to allow trading room and still be under the support. In the event it breaks support, it will also break the 200 DMA. And that is a definite historical sign of weakness.

Stopped Out!

Trade review

After being in the trade for about eight months, our stop loss has once again taken us out and our money is safely in our account. Let's see what we missed after we were taken out by our stop loss.

The support at $125 did not hold although the stock tried to stay above it. As you can see the stock traded down to the support on August 2, 2011 and held. But the next day it traded below it, which took us out of the trade, before closing back above the support that day. But that didn't last long.

See Figure 16f following.

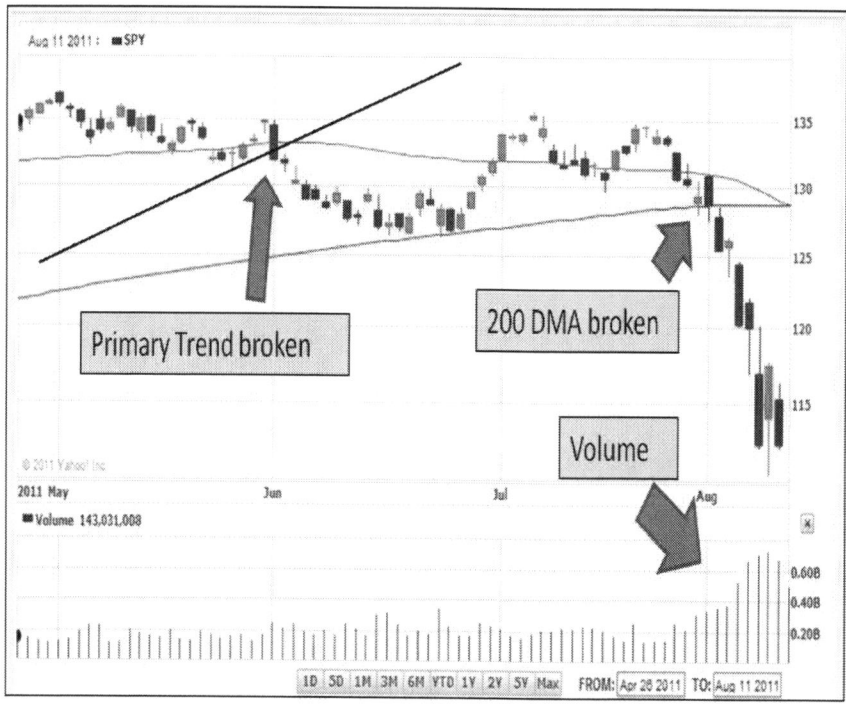

Figure 16f

The volume increased dramatically once the stock broke below the 200 DMA causing a decline of more than $10 per share and below our purchase price. There is no way of knowing if this decline is a market correction or something more significant such as the beginning of a bear market.

We do know by the price and volume action of our stock (SPY) this looks to be a classic topping of the market. The last two highs were lower, giving the indication the market *is rolling over*. Also the higher volume on declines and the lower volume on advances is yet another sign of topping out.

Trading the Trends

This particular advance began at $102 per share and reached a high of about $135 per share, a $33 advance. To decline back to $112, as the chart shows, is a $21 fall and is much more than the normal correction of 30% to 50% of the preceding advance.

We do know this much: We are not a part of it. If it falls another $20, $40, $60 or more, we will simply sit and watch. In two trades during a time span of two years we made a total profit of about 35% on our investments and protected our capital every step of the way. I would have preferred to have made more than we did, but that's all the market gave us.

We will continue to watch for another low-risk opportunity with the potential for high return. But as of this writing, we are current with the market. As trend lines are broken and moving averages are violated, the market changes and so do the trends. But it is not always resuming the previous advance or entering a decline. Sometimes the new trend is a range-bound sideways trend, both long-term and short-term.

> When I'm bearish and I sell a stock, each sale must be at a lower level than the previous sale. When I am buying, the reverse is true. I must buy on a rising scale. I don't buy long stocks on a scale down, I buy on a scale up.
> ~Jesse Livermore

©Copyright McAllen Publishing

Chapter 15

Trading Sideways

The 3-trend market only has one long-term phase that either advances or declines, the public participation phase. Although that phase can last from several months to several years, it leaves out large timeframes of opportunities to add capital to the investing account. And we like money!

The distribution and accumulation phases can last for several months and also offer many profitable trading opportunities. However, the trading is shorter term and higher risk. These market phases are sideways and the trading strategies for sideways trends are a little different.

The Two Approaches

You can usually classify trading indicators into one of two approaches, the confirming approach and the predictive approach.

Trading the Trends

The first approach is a **confirming approach**, and this one is what we have been using in the long-term trades. By using technical analysis, using confirmations such as waiting for the stock to trade back across the 200 DMA or trading above the trend line and close to support before entering a trade, we are placing as many odds in our favor as possible to confirm the future direction of the stock. By using powerful indicators and entering very close to known support, this approach produces very low-risk trades and is very effective.

The second approach is a **predictive approach**. Rather than being confirming, this approach predicts that a move has begun, sometimes prior to having some other indicator confirming the move.

Quite often, this approach uses recent market movement, such as a low that has been reached, and technical analysis to predict a short-term trend has reversed and conditions have changed.

The two approaches, **predictive** and **confirming**, will sometimes give conflicting signals when analyzing price movements of the same time domain. That is okay because they are used for different purposes and have different goals. For instance, if the market has reached a bottom over the intermediate term, the confirming approach almost always indicates that the trend is still down. This is normal, because as prices are plummeting or near a low, the large price drop makes the trend indicators such as the trend line and the moving averages point down. But at the same time, the predictive approach may be showing that the end of the decline has been reached and higher prices are ahead.

©Copyright McAllen Publishing

There are times it is beneficial to use both approaches, which is what we have done in earlier trades. Interestingly, even if you use the predictive approach, you will still need the confirmations used in the confirming approach eventually. For instance, maybe the market has traded down severely and reached a potential bottom. By using the predictive approach, you might see strong volume on a few up days, and the down days do not produce a lower low. The confirming approach would still be waiting for a higher low or some other indicator to confirm the bottom is in place.

However, buying at an apparent low would be predicting the market is about to move higher. In the event it did, the confirmations such as a higher low, the higher high, and the moving averages would come later.

This may sound a bit like picking a bottom. And if traded haphazardly, it would be. However, there are certain technical indicators that can predict a change in price movement such as reaching a prior support level, or DOJI or Engulfing candles that form after a decline. The keys are, *waiting for the indicators to form*, and waiting for enough of them to form to be reasonably sure of a buy signal.

As an example, the following chart shows the stock trading below the 200 DMA, has been in a decline, and would not be a trade using the confirming approach. And according to this chart, there are also more than three months of trading opportunities when the market is moving sideways, as it has yet to find a new direction either up or down.

Trading the Trends   173

So let's look at three different trading opportunities to buy short term and capture some profit on a bounce.

See Figure 12g following.

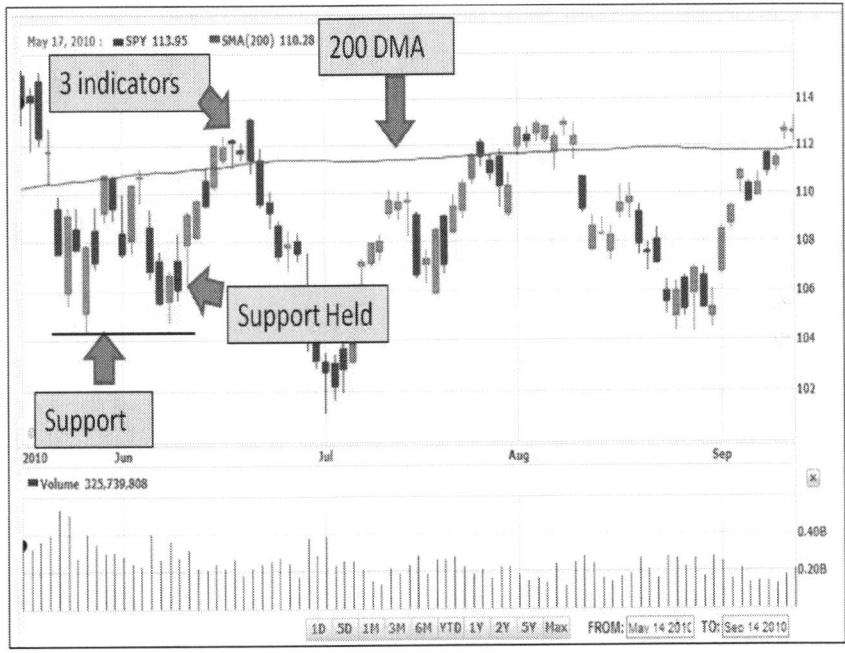

Figure 12g

The first trading opportunity on the above chart shows the stock made a low on the left side of the chart, and then tested that low about two weeks later and the support held. When it tested the low, the early indicator is a positive trading day above the prior support. The following day was a negative day, yet it closed above the low of the two previous trading days. The support had then held three consecutive days following at least a 5-day decline. Buying on the third or fourth day at $106 would allow a risk of $2 with a stop loss just under the support. This is using a predictive approach. Although there is nothing indicating a trend change, these are indicators predicting a bounce. In this case it bounced from the $106 entry point to above $112 for a $6 gain.

Know when to get out! Short-term trading is different from long-term. While trading long term following an advancing trend, we moved our stop loss up to the next known support. Short-term trading is different. It requires knowing when to take your money and run. In a sideways trend any pullback may be right back down to your entry point or lower. So you don't give it time to take back your profits.

In this trade there is more than a 5-day advance, so it's likely time for a pullback. Then there are three indicators at the top that are very good predictors of an impending decline.

First of all, the stock trades four days unable to break above the first high of that advance. In those four days, three negative daily candles formed. In technical analysis, any of these three particular candles that form at the top of an advance are very good predictors of a decline in the near future.

The first one of these three is the candle with a long wick and a small body top. At the bottom, after a decline, that candle is called a 'hammer.' But at the top after an advance it is called a 'hanging man.' The second negative candle is called a 'spinning top,' and the third is called a 'bearish engulfing' candle. When any of these three form at the top after an advance, it is your warning a decline may be about to happen. And in this case all three are there. It's time to run.

©Copyright McAllen Publishing

This trade would have lasted about a week. It was semi-low risk using the predictive approach to trading with technical analysis. A trade was not made on the first decline on the left side of the chart because there was only one candle indicating a bottom. A trade there would have been high risk.

Let's look at the next trade.

See Figure 12e below.

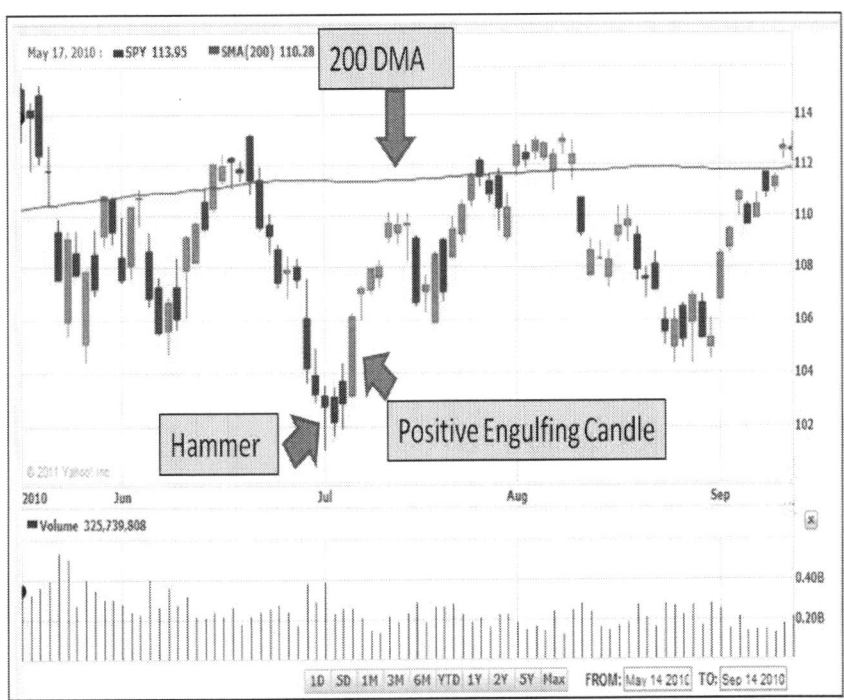

Figure 12e

The above chart shows at the end of an 8-day decline the stock found support at the $102 level. It traded four days under $104 and closed higher on the fourth day. The following day the positive engulfing candle was further confirmation of support.

Entering on that positive day in the $104 to $105 range would be semi-low risk with a stop loss under $102, just a couple of dollars away. That way we are only stepping in *after* a decline and still minimizing any possible loss by using a stop loss just below the entry point.

Again, know when to get out. With a $6 to $8 gain after a 5-day advance, you should be anticipating a pullback. And in a sideways market, there is no way of knowing where the bottom will be. That's why it is imperative to wait for each bottom to show signs of holding instead of trying to pick a bottom. Let's look at one more trade from this chart.

The third trade is another that is entered under the 200 DMA while using technical analysis to find an entry point. First, let's address the pause in the middle of the decline leading to this trade.

The stock made that first low on only one negative trading day. There are two gaps in trading, and even though one might anticipate those gaps being filled, a one-day decline is not an entry point. The safer trades are always at the end of a decline, and preferably, after at least a 5-day decline with positive trading days indicating at least minor support at that level.

See Figure 12f following.

Figure 12f

This trade follows an almost 30-day decline with the stock showing support at $104, which is also very close to the support on our first trade.

There are six trading days, three of which are positive, and it never closed below $104.50. This would be a low-risk opportunity, entering on the third or fourth day at $105 with a stop loss just below $104. This is a minimum-risk trade with a potential for good return.

During this trade, with an $8 to $10 profit after at least a 5-day advance, don't be greedy. You should get out, move your stop loss up, or use a trailing stop loss to preserve your profit in the event of a decline. When trading sideways, a decline is both anticipatory and technical. Following an advance you should be anticipating a pullback or correction while at the same time watching for obvious signs of weakness. Signs of weakness include resistance at the 200 DMA, the formation of a spinning-top candle, or a bearish engulfing candle.

When trading in a sideways market, there are four criteria each trade must meet. These trades are buying pullbacks, so in order to buy:

1. Enter *only* after a decline of at least five days.
2. Enter *only* after signs of support. (two to four days trading at that level with positive trading days)
3. Stop loss must be very close to entry point.
4. Know your target price. Make sure the stock has headroom, and be ready to exit at the target price or have a trailing stop loss do it for you.

When these criteria are met, the predictive approach can be implemented to capture short-term gains while holding any losses to a minimum.

This approach can be used at a market top during the distribution phase, at a market bottom during the accumulation phase, or in advancing and declining markets as well. The two most important trading rules continue to be:

1. Always use a stop loss
2. Always protect your capital

Trading the Trends

By entering only when the criteria are met, you are showing patience to let the market come to you. You won't have to search for some signal hidden deep in an hourly or 5-minute chart that might suggest something that's not really there. When the opportunities arise, they will be clear. Using a 3-month chart and watching the closing prices is helpful. Look for any support/resistance and wait for the opportunity.

During sideways or declining markets, many investors choose to sit on their money. But for some, this is another opportunity to make money. The risk is higher; it is more difficult to be right, so some offset the potential loss in trading higher risk by trading a smaller number of shares. But you must do what you are comfortable with and what works for you.

Let's learn how **Trading the Trends** can be just as effective in recognizing a declining trend and profit as the trend moves lower.

> "The market does not beat them. They beat themselves, because though they have brains they cannot sit tight."
> ~Jesse Livermore

Chapter 16

The Stinking Market

For the buy-and-hold investor, a declining market is nothing shy of a living nightmare. During the bear market from 2007 to 2009 many investors refused to open their investment account statements to avoid the emotional distress of looking at the declining balance. Although that might help preserve the emotions a bit, the sticking your head in the sand approach is about as silly as allowing such a loss to happen in the first place.

But for some, they were doing as their financial advisor suggested. It's true, some financial advisors actually suggested to their clients to not open the statements. Of course, they also assured those clients, "The market always comes back." Well, does it?

The point is, most investors who were sold investments at the market highs in 2000 or in 2007 are still waiting to break even. As of this writing, those investors have waited 11 years and four years, respectively. And they continue to wait. I seriously doubt they were expecting to lose money for so many years *waiting for the market to come back*.

But historically, bear markets last an average of nearly two years and then it takes another couple of years for the market to get back to net-gain territory. And secular bear markets have historically lasted 17 to 20 years, and there's no reason to think the one starting in 2000 will be any different.

So what do we do when the market heads south? Well, there are several ways to make money using many of the same techniques we've already learned. We have to adjust our thinking a bit, but fortunately that's usually not a problem.

Making money in a declining market can be done by:

1. **Short selling stocks or the indexes like SPY, QQQ, or DIA**
2. **Buying PUT options on stocks or indexes**
3. **Earning interest on your money**

And for the investor who hates to watch his balance decline but just can't sell out and move to safety:

4. **Sell covered call options on stock he/she is holding**

This list is certainly not complete or comprehensive, but these are the simplest ways to make money during market declines while protecting your capital. We won't waste your time on ways to draw interest on your money, but we will take the other strategies one at a time, protect our capital at all times, and learn to profit even when the market stinks.

First we have to recognize a market top and impending decline as it is starting. Since all stocks follow the broader market up and down, we keep our eye on the overall market by using the SPY.

By using trends and technical analysis we can project what the market may do in the near term and learn to adjust our strategies to take advantage of the opportunities it gives us. Much like we did in the previous advancing market, by using trend and channel lines we could predict future lows and future highs. So let's start with recognizing market weakness since that is the first thing that happens at market tops and is our first red flag.

The early signs of market weakness and possibly a change in the primary trend are classic. There are five things an investor and trader should always be on the lookout for. Obviously the main culprits are:

- **Lower volume on advances**
- **Higher volume on declines**
- **Inability to make higher highs**
- **Primary trend line broken**
- **200 DMA broken**

Although it is not always the case, these are listed in the order they normally occur.

Trading the Trends

Looking back at the market high in 2007 in the following chart, these same occurrences at the market high led to that decimating bear market. As you know, these are exactly the same technical break-downs that took us out of our last trade in 2011.

See Figure 17 following

Figure 17

The 2007-2008 break-down was not an isolated incident by any means. But look closely at the first high in July 2007. It was on increased volume and that is good but then the decline hit and the volume skyrockets. The highest high was then made on low volume. Not good. Any investor or trader who was still in the market after the trend line and 200 DMA were broken got a gift. A new market high with the warning from the market gods yelling, "Low volume, get out!" This gift was the golden opportunity to sell at the highs and let some novice take the loss.

When the first high was higher but did not reach the upper channel line, that was the first red flag. And simply applying the technique of using the two previous highs to adjust the channel line as additional highs form, it shows in graphic detail the market just *rolling over*.

That same technique works every time. Let's look at the early market weakness and break-down of the market high in 2000-2001. See Figure 17a following.

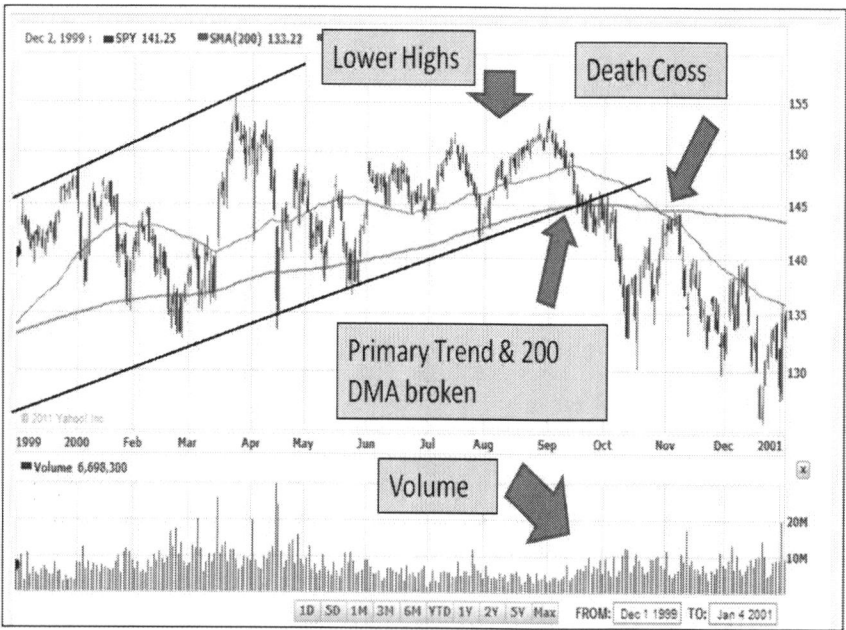

Figure 17a

The preceding chart and the previous chart are strikingly similar. The market tops in 2001 and 2007 show the same technical break-downs, the breaking below the primary trend line, below the 200 DMA, lower highs, and increased volume on the declines. By using the two previous highs technique, the channel line could be adjusted and would clearly show the market rolling over.

The preceding chart also includes the *death cross*.

The death cross is a term used when the 50 DMA drops below the 200 DMA. The 50 DMA normally stays above the 200 DMA but will cross the 200 DMA at times during other market corrections so it is not always the tell-tale sign of all things heading lower. But after an extended market advance, one should already be anticipating a change in trend anyway, so when the death cross appears at a market high it should certainly get, and hold, your attention.

Some skeptics may think watching a market roll over in what appears to be slow motion is much easier than a market crash. Market crashes can send stock prices plummeting. Many think a crash happens suddenly and without warning, so there's no way to predict it.

Sorry, but the skeptics are wrong again. There are warning signs. Let's take a look at the Black Monday crash in 1987.

Trading the Trends

Many of the classic signs were there. There was a weaker high that couldn't reach the upper channel line in August, a lower high by October 1, crossing the 200 DMA, and breaking the primary trend line. Four warnings before Black Monday arrived.

See Figure 17-1 below.

Figure 17-1

The market was speaking, was anyone listening? For some, it obviously was not yelling loud enough. Let's take a closer look and see just how much time a Trend Trader would have had to get out and avoid the crash.

The lower high was made more than a week before the crash. The primary trend line was broken 5 days before the crash and the 200 DMA was broken three days before. See Figure 17-2 below.

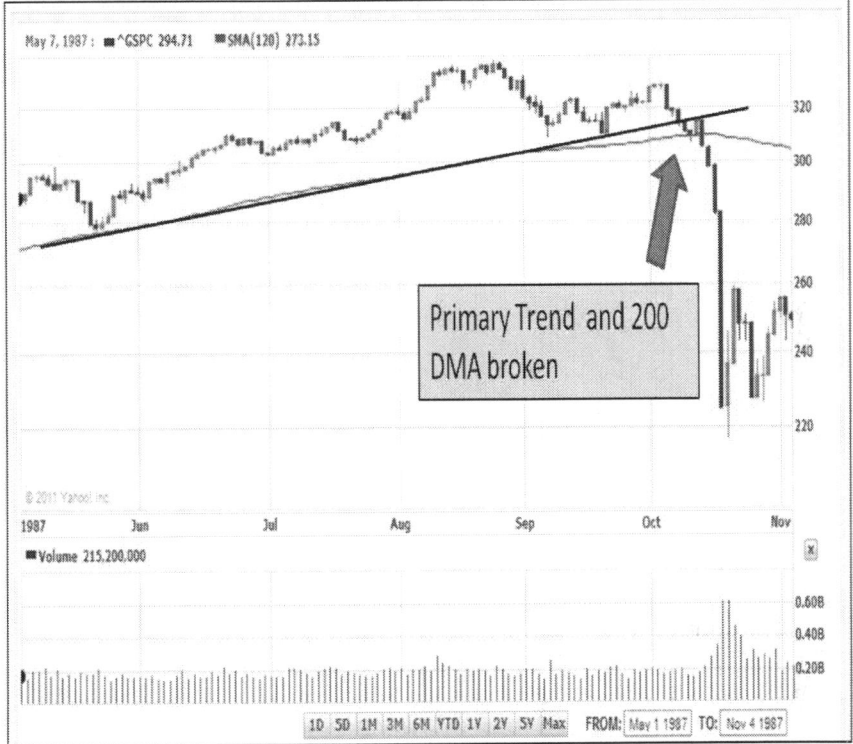

Figure 17-2

An astute investor or trader wouldn't need more than three warnings before exiting. If someone wanted additional confirmation, then a support/resistance line drawn across the two lows made in September would have also shown the market breaking that support the day after it broke the primary trend line. Let that be a lesson. Keeping the stop loss under known support is important.

These similarities are nothing new. Let's look back one more time. The market decline beginning in 1973 leading to a brutal bear market began with the exact same technical breakdowns. See Figure 17b below.

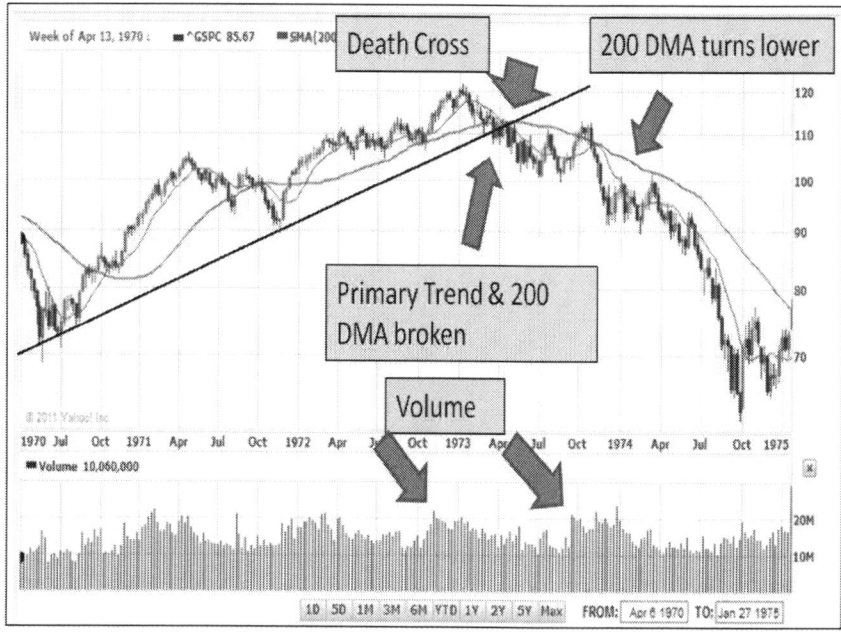

Figure 17b

History does repeat itself and technical analysis is the key to recognizing a change in trend *as* it is happening. It is a matter of following defined trading and investing rules to avoid major losses.

Trading the Trends

Determining a new trend from the top is the same as we did from the bottom. We need two significant highs and two significant lows, and then we can draw our trend and channel lines. Obviously for the trend to change, the most recent high would be lower than the previous high and the most recent low would be lower than the previous low. These are the early indicators that a new trend is developing. When the stock can no longer make a higher high, it is weak. When it can no longer make a higher low, then this confirms the weakness.

Let's take a look at the current market as of August 2011. See Figure 17d below.

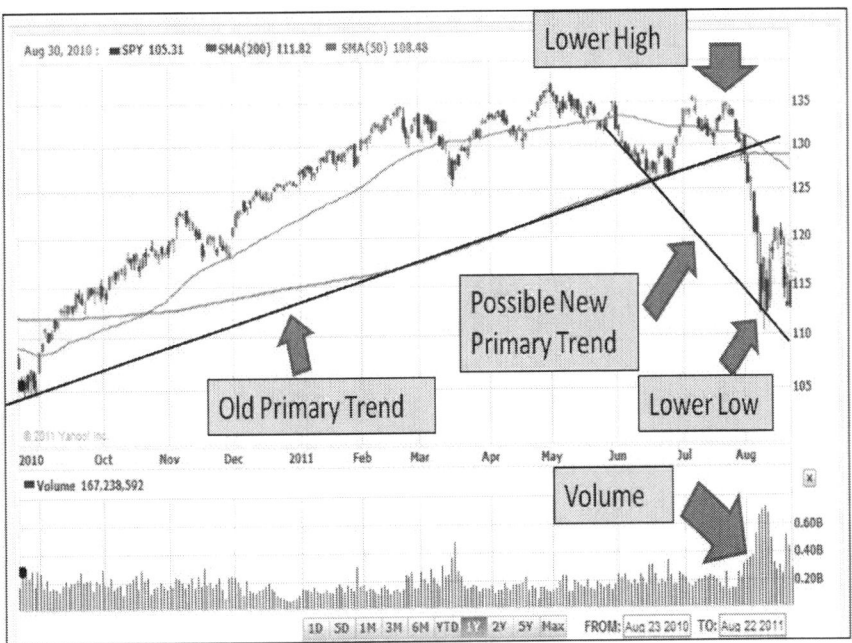

Figure 17d

©Copyright McAllen Publishing

First of all, you can see the same tell-tale signs of possible primary trend change, just as history has taught us to recognize. We have the technical breakdowns including the death cross, lower highs, a lower low, and increased volume on the declines. The lower low is already in place, but a significant lower high has yet to develop. So confirmation of a new trend is still pending.

When the market speaks, it pays to listen. The charts do not lie. Every tell-tale sign of a change in trend are present. This is why we sold out when our technical indicators said to leave. We are not going to argue with the market. And we are going to protect our capital at all times.

When we have confirming lows or highs, we will trade accordingly using trends, channels, moving averages, and technical analysis to make informed decisions. But at this point, our money is safe in our account until the market tells us which way it will go.

Since a second low or high has yet to form in 2011, let's use the decline from the high in 2000 as an example of the steps we take in determining a new trend from a market top. These will be exactly the same steps taken on the current market as additional lows and highs form, and on future markets as well.

See figure 17c following.

Trading the Trends

Figure 17c

The above chart shows the changing trend as it was happening. The final high was made on September 1, 2000, and was lower than the highest high. This was the first red flag. The following decline created a lower low. This low was lower than the two previous lows which was another indicator of a primary trend change to be added to the propensity of evidence, specifically, the breaking of the trend line and breaking below the 200 DMA.

The stock made a triple top. And as we discussed in one of our early trades when the stock made a double bottom that was a positive sign. It was possibly retesting the lows. A double or triple top is the opposite. It is testing the highs but can't move higher. So it is a negative, and also an indicator that a decline is ahead. The third high on the right side was not as high as the first. This was another sign of weakness. But then the lower low developed within 45 days of that last high, giving the Trend Trader a point to draw a trend line. If further confirmation was desired, then another lower high formed about 30 days later. Thus, within about 60 days from the market high the Trend Trader already had the necessary information to determine a new primary trend and channel.

For the conservative who wanted further confirmation, he/she only had to wait about 30 more days for the next lower high to develop. Thus, by early December 2000, just about three months from the market high, the trend is confirmed.

Yes, these are the early stages of a primary trend. But primary trends historically last much more than 90 days, and secondary trends normally do not last that long. So, in any event, whether this could possibly have been just a secondary trend and would soon resume the previous advance or confirmation of a new primary trend, to the Trend Trader, it doesn't really matter. We are going to protect our capital in the early stages of a trend the same as we do in the later stages.

So any trade initiated upon confirmation of a possible new declining primary trend would have all the same safeguards to protect our capital as any other trade. Yet, when the evidence points to a decline, our strategies will change with the market.

The important things you should recognize in the early stages of a primary trend change at a market top are always the same.

1. **Lower highs and lower lows**
2. **Higher volume on declines**
3. **Technical breakdown (below trend line and 200 DMA)**
4. **Low volume on advances**

These are classic signs and just the mirror image of a trend change at the end of a declining trend. When the next advance is beginning there are higher highs, increased volume on advances, breakouts above the channel line and the 200 DMA. Recognizing the change is the first order of business, what we do with that information is next.

When changing trends, the market doesn't just send one signal. There is no Holy Grail; one single indicator or event that will give everyone forewarning by telling all investors the trend is changing. It is a matter of using the appropriate tools to recognize the early signs, taking the propensity of evidence, and recognizing one more indicator when it happens and adding it to the list. Once you have seen two or three warning signs, no more information is needed.

Novices, who buy market tops, lose. The market sends them the same warnings, but it's like the driver of the car in front of them turns their left blinker on but the novice attempts to pass them anyway. The wise investor does not need the driver in front of them to also stick their hand out the window and scream. When the market speaks, we listen.

Chapter 17

Trading the Downtrend

Trading successfully in a declining market has some variations to the strategies we've already used while trading the previous advance. For some, it's backwards thinking. Instead of the typical *buy low, sell high* mindset that seems to come natural for most, declining markets require us to think just the opposite, *sell high, buy low.*

Some folks have great difficulty bringing themselves to trade in the downtrend. And for those sitting on the sidelines with their money in the account safe from risk, that is just fine. But let me shed a little more light on the subject before you decide how you want to invest or trade in declining markets. You see, the market always falls faster than it advances. We will use this known fact in trading in options later, but for now, let's take a look at short selling.

Short Selling the Trend

Short selling is one of the strategies to make money in a declining market that I mentioned earlier. Most people have heard about short selling but never took the time to learn the ins and outs of it. Many also develop a negative opinion about it and decide not to learn. But short selling is certainly a way to make money in a declining market while using the same rules to protect our capital.

The only difference is we are selling at the highs and buying back at the lows, and keeping the difference as profit.

To make it simple, I'll give you a quick overview and then we'll place a trade. Seeing how it is done makes it easier to understand, but you need to know the basics first.

When you set up an account with your broker, there are two kinds of accounts. A cash account and a margin account. A cash account requires that you pay for your stock when you make the purchase, but with a margin account the broker can lend you a portion of the funds at the time of purchase and the security acts as collateral. This also gives you the ability to buy more stock with the same dollars. For example, if you had $50,000 in a cash account, then you could buy $50,000 worth of stock. But that $50,000 in a margin account allows you to buy about $100,000 worth of stock.

NOTE: Trading on margin, buying twice as much stock as you have cash to cover, is added risk. I would not advise doing it unless you are an experienced trader. For making trades like we have done so far, either type of account would work fine.

But in order to make short sale trades you must have a margin account. Now, this does not mean we have to trade in more stock than we have cash for. But for short selling, a margin account is required.

When an investor goes long on an investment, it means that he or she has bought a stock believing its price will rise in the future. Conversely, when an investor goes short, he or she is anticipating a decrease in share price.

I am sure at some time you've seen a stock that you were certain was overpriced or had advanced to some unsustainable level. You probably thought nobody in their right mind would be buying that stock at that price and you were certain it would fall. That's what short selling allows you to do. Take advantage of those opportunities and make money when it does fall.

Short selling is the selling of a stock that the seller doesn't own. More specifically, a short sale is the sale of a security that isn't owned by the seller, but that is promised to be delivered. That may sound confusing, but it's actually a simple concept. And the transaction is all electronic and handled by your broker so it's not like you have to do anything other than place the trade.

Are you still with me? Here's the skinny: when you short sell a stock, your broker will lend the shares to you for you to sell without you actually owning them. The stock will come from the brokerage's own inventory, from another one of the firm's customers, or from another brokerage firm.

The shares are then sold by you, just as if you actually owned them, and the proceeds are credited to your margin account. Sooner or later, you must "close" the short sale by buying back the same number of shares (called covering) and returning them to your broker.

Again, this is all done electronically. If the price drops, as you suspect, you can buy back the stock at the lower price and make a profit on the difference simply by placing the trade.

If the price of the stock rises, you have to buy it back at the higher price than you sold it for, and you lose money.

So it is the opposite of buying low and selling high. You are selling high and buying low. But you do have to buy it back. Remember, because you don't own the stock you're short selling (you borrowed and then sold it), you must buy it back to return the borrowed shares.

Short selling does have risks that buying stock does not have. For instance, if you buy a stock the most you can lose is your investment. If SPY had dropped to $0.00 and was totally worthless, without any stop loss protection, the most we could have lost was our original investment of $90,000.

But if we are short selling a stock, the price could possibly go up to the infinite. So if we shorted the stock at $90 per share and it advanced to $300 per share, without a stop loss placed above our purchase price for protection, we would lose $210,000.

Simply because we have to buy the stock back, allowing a stock price to go against you is not a smart thing to do. But that is an exaggerated example.

That is what scares most people. But that is also what stop losses are for, to protect our capital. Let's use the 2000 trend change and short sell the SPY. Placing a trade will give you a better understanding.

See Figure 18 below.

Figure 18

Once the first lower high is formed, we could draw our declining upper channel line. This lower high stopped at the 200 DMA and could not trade above it. By extending our channel line we would know when the stock advanced back up to it and confirm the new trend. After the second lower low, SPY traded higher to $140 per share but began another decline. This lower high at $140 was the third high; it touched our upper channel line, and was our confirmation of a trend change. This also told us that $140 was a resistance level.

This information allows us to place a trade very close to known resistance and place a stop loss just above the resistance of $140.

The following day we sold 1000 shares short at $138 per share.

Done!

We have now sold short. It's time to place our stop loss. Or in this case, a buy stop.

Knowing there is resistance at $140, we will place our buy stop at $141, just above the resistance level. As you can see, this is backwards from our earlier trades. We were buying at support and placing our stop loss under the support level. Now we are selling at resistance and placing our buy stop above the known resistance in the event the stock advances and goes against us.

The Buy Stop

The stop loss for a short sale is a bit different. It's called a **Buy Stop**. This means simply in the event the stock trades up to $141, then we would buy the stock back to close the trade.

The trade to buy would be executed automatically just like our stop loss was initiated to take us out of the previous trades.

To explain; a *Buy Stop* type of stop loss can be used for more than one purpose. For instance, if you were watching a stock trade up to a resistance level but you didn't want to buy it until it had the strength to trade higher through resistance, then you could use a Buy Stop.

Your trade would then only be executed when the stock traded up to your target level. It works the same when using the Buy Stop to exit a short sale position.

We placed the Buy Stop at $141 because we do not want to buy the stock back unless it reaches $141, and as long as the stock trades lower than that level we are still in the trade. We will only be stopped out if the stock advances to our stop price.

Once again, do ***not*** get creative with your buy stop (stop loss), specifically adding a limit trigger. By adding a limit trigger, our order would then be called a **Buy Stop Limit**.

Currently, if the stock advances to $141, then our order is executed, the shares are purchased at Market Price, and we are out of the trade.

But using a Buy Stop Limit, we would order the purchase of the shares but limit the amount per share we paid to, let's say, less than $141.50. In other words, if the stock traded up to $141, then the stop would be triggered but the trade would *not* be executed unless the stock could be purchased lower than the limit that was set. If this stock were to shoot up right through $141 per share, gap up above that amount, whatever, you want out. Period. End of Story.

Just like our previous trades, if it fell through support, we wanted out. No hanging on hoping, wishing, and praying. Just get out. Protect the capital at all times.

So do not use a buy stop limit order. Keep it simple with a buy stop. If the stock trades to $141, we want out at the market price, even if that happens to be $141.90 or $142. We would rather take a little extra loss and be out of the trade. We never allow the market the opportunity to turn any investment or trade into a huge loss whether we are trading an advancing or declining market.

Let's see how the short sale worked out. At the time of the trade we would only have had the information to draw the channel line as it is indicated on the chart below. The next lower high at $138 was not formed prior to our trade.

See Figure 18a following.

Figure 18a

After we sold it short, the stock dropped close to $15 per share, traded back higher but never reached $140 per share, and never reached our buy stop of $141.

Yet after that last high at $138 the trend line would have been redrawn to include that new high. Also, after that last high at $138, it was *lights out!* All downhill from there!

Stocks do fall faster than they rise. In most charts you can see the advances take their time working their way up, but declines can be sharp and severe. That is classic market movement.

Let's move ahead in time and see what happened. See Figure 18b following.

Trading the Trends 203

Figure 18b

You'll notice in the preceding chart I didn't include a lower trend line, only the upper channel line. We wouldn't care how far it fell, we would really only be concerned with it staying below the upper channel line and our short sale price and/or buy stop. The lower trend line would be needed if you were intending to cover the short sale at a low. The stock continued to trend lower following our sale in December 2000 until it broke out above the channel line in April 2003.

Managing the trade on the short sale simply means we would have moved our buy stop down every time the stock bounced and created a lower high. That lower high would have been new resistance and a place for our buy stop.

Needless to say, we could have stayed short for about 27 months and bought the shares back to close the trade at about $90 per share or less. Or in other words, about a $50,000 profit.

In our early trades, we were following the stock higher. Many traders would have been tempted to take the profit when the stock traded up to the channel line, wait for it to return to the lower trend line and reenter. Following a stock lower is the mirror image. When a stock falls to the lower trend line, or possibly beyond the lower trend, it is always tempting to take the profit and run. This is a trader's personal decision. But in a declining trend it may be a wise decision. Because unlike in an uptrend, most of the time in a declining trend a drop can be sharp, severe, and can happen quickly. During these times it can be panic selling and covering a short position can be a huge profit. So take what the market gives.

Short setup

Now that you have an understanding of the basics of selling short, let's look closer at finding entry and exit points.

Entering a short position (selling) is very similar to entering a long position (buying). In our first trades, we were stopped out when the stock dropped below the primary trend line, which at the time was also very close to the 200 DMA. We initially entered those trades after the stock showed the strength to trade above the 200 DMA and the primary trend line. Selling short is just the opposite.

We are looking for opportunities that include the following characteristics:

1. **The primary trend is declining (trading *with* the trend)**
2. **Stock is unable to trade above the 200 DMA, is trading close to, and under the channel line**
3. **The stock is trading close to resistance (Buy Stop close to short sale price, minimum capital risk)**

Let's find a good setup. First, we must look at the big picture. So I started with a 2-year chart to find the long-term primary trend. Then I narrowed our time frame down to a 1-year chart. The following is a 1-year chart which has the long-term primary trend extended from the 2-year chart.

See Figure 18c following.

Figure 18c

The above chart is of the SPY showing the primary trend change in late 2007. When the market is topping out and the trend is changing, from a trader or investor's perspective there are several strategies to use when given the above scenario.

Remember, this is the distribution phase of the market cycle as the primary trend is changing. So there are wider trading range days, more volatility, and more movement. It is a much different market than the narrow trading range days during the public participation phase when slow advances were common.

At a market top, there are experienced investors selling and moving to safety, and some are likely allocating a portion of their capital to switch sides of the market and go short, so some of the selling pressure is short sales. There are novices buying tops and every little pullback thinking the market will go up forever. There are those who Dollar Cost Average, so they are foolishly buying regardless what the market is doing or may be about to do.

Your trading and investing style is your own. You must do what you are comfortable with. You may want confirmation before stepping in or you may want to tip-toe in by buying or selling small increments. That is your decision.

The Growling Bear

Some traders are just bears. It's as simple as that. They growl at every market advance. Instead of looking for support and buying at a low to take advantage of an advance, they are constantly waiting for an advance so they can sell. Needless to say, they are always selling tops, using a buy stop to protect their capital, and looking for the decline. There is wisdom in this strategy.

Since the market always falls faster than it advances, their profit often comes quickly. When viewing the preceding chart as it formed, the aggressive bear would have sold the very top, or at a minimum sold short after the very next advance that didn't reach the previous high. The less aggressive bear would have waited for the first low to develop and sold short on the next high or as the price dropped below the 200 DMA.

The Conservative Bull

The conservative bull is the investor who likes confirmation. He doesn't want to jump in, or out, too early. But looking at the preceding chart, surely even the most conservative of bulls would have moved to safety at some point. If not when the primary trend line was broken, then maybe after the stock made a lower high, and certainly when it was unable to trade back up above the 200 DMA. Those were three blatant warning signs. The same warning signs that appear at all market tops.

Yes, you can pull up historical charts of every long term market advance, apply a trend line, and when the advance fell below the primary trend line would have been the time to exit. Many times the broken primary trend is the first sign of the beginning of a bear market.

The Perma-Bull

Besides the growling bear and the conservative bull, there are the perma-bulls who stay fully invested. They see a 100-year chart like the one earlier in Market History and are willing to wait as long as it takes for profit. So, for the perma-bull, don't worry, I will show you how to protect your capital without ever selling a single share of stock. Just hang on, we'll get there.

Let's pinpoint an entry to sell short using only the information we would have had available on the day of sale. We have done the necessary preparation by looking at the big picture. There is a significant lower low and the trend and moving averages have been broken. It's time to take a closer look.

Trading the Trends 209

See Figure 18d below.

Figure 18d

First of all, for a closer look I normally use a 3-month chart, as I have done here. It is a personal preference, mainly because the 3-month chart gives a very good picture of most secondary and minor trends on the same chart, and at the same time, it condenses the noise and smaller movements that are often confusing when trying to use a 5-day or 1-month chart. The 3-month chart provides an accurate medium-size picture, so to speak.

As of the last trading day shown at the far-right of the chart, let's analyze the information we have. We'll take the positives first.

1. The possible new primary trend line is declining and is rapidly approaching the 200 DMA from above.

2. The stock has already traded up to the new possible trend line two times since the highest high and could not trade higher.

3. The stock had traded up to the current high of $149 about 30 days ago and fell. So this level is already known resistance.

4. Yesterday, according to the second candle from the right, the stock closed above the 200 DMA but was on very low volume.

5. It advanced for five days to yesterday's high, then closed lower, and below the 200 DMA today (possibly ready to trade lower for three to five days).

6. Currently the stock is at $148 and there is known resistance just one dollar away. The next higher resistance is at $152, just $3 away (very low risk).

Now the negatives.

1. There is minor support below the current price at $144 that was tested just 30 days ago.

2. The next level of support is at $140.

There are never any perfect setups, but we use the information available to make an informed decision.

Trading the Trends

In doing so, we only put our money at risk when the odds of success are in our favor.

Now, I'm not going to waste your time following this trade down, as we already know what happens. It never trades back above the trade short-sale price and eventually drops more than 50% to less than $70 per share. So the math is easy. The key to finding a good entry point is just the opposite as when we were buying.

1. Wait for the stock to advance. Preferably close to a resistance level, the declining trend line, or the 200 DMA. That allows the buy stop to be above that resistance and very close to the entry. That keeps your risk exposure to a minimum (low risk, possible high return).

2. Remember the 3 – 5 market. This is correct more times than it's not. Thus, the advance prior to a short-sale should fit into one of these trading timelines, and preferably the 5-day variety.

3. Use the buy stop. Never place a trade before you know exactly where the buy stop will be and how much you are risking, and *do not leave your computer until you have placed the buy stop.*

Once you are in a profitable position, continue to adjust your trend and channel lines when necessary. In a short sale, always keep your buy stop just above known resistance. Move it lower as needed, and be ready to buy back the shares to close the sale when the stock breaks out above the upper channel line. That is usually your first clue the primary trend is changing. While we are discussing short sales, you need to be aware of the short squeeze.

The short squeeze

As you can imagine, when a stock begins a decline there will be many traders entering a short position. Then during the decline, temporary support levels are found and the stock rallies back higher. This creates the movement that shows up as stair-steps on the chart.

Many times these temporary bottoms are made because the stock has reached an over-sold level. This could be in relation to the current economic conditions.

Meaning, the economy is headed into a downturn, but hasn't declined enough yet to warrant a complete sell-off. Thus, the market adjusts by moving a bit higher, because *the market discounts everything*. So in the event the economy held at that particular level, and there is a chance it could, the market does not immediately sell off to unwarranted levels. So the decline may have reached an oversold level and a bounce brings the prices back in line with current conditions.

Another cause for a bounce or a bear market rally is the short squeeze. To explain, when the short interest in a stock becomes high, buying interest may help a stock find temporary support. As the stock begins to advance, the short-sellers begin buying to lock in their gains. As more buying occurs, the stock price continues to advance, causing more short sellers to buy in fear of losing their gains, or possibly incurring a loss if the stock price advances too far.

There are other times when the short interest is high on a stock and large buyers such as a hedge fund might see the high short interest and begin buying. Their buying causes the advance, and it has a snowball effect. As they buy, more and more short sellers are forced to buy to cover their positions. Then the large buyer would sell into the advance for a profit. This action is called a short *squeeze* because it is squeezing the short sellers and forcing them to buy at higher prices.

When the price is rapidly advancing, these short sellers have no idea when, or if, it will stop going up. So to prevent major loss they are forced to buy the stock to cover their short sale. If they already have buy stop losses in place, then those are triggered and filled. The more buying to cover, the more rapid the advance.

The short squeeze actually generates excellent conditions for new short sales. The covering rally cleans out buying pressure and restores balance. Upside momentum ebbs and the environment that generated selling in the first place suddenly returns. Market players sense this and quickly reverse the short-term trend.

One thing to remember is: In a declining market, a rally should not exceed 50 to 60% of the prior fall unless strong buyers enter the action.

This is the exact opposite of an advancing market when the declines shouldn't exceed 30% to 50% of the previous advance.

Short squeezes rarely break above major resistance like the 200 DMA or the declining primary trend. More than likely, only the novices with very bad trading skills and no experience buy stocks as they watch the market rise. They are afraid *"The train is leaving the station without them"* and jump on.

You should always avoid selling short into strongly negative momentum. Your risk escalates dramatically when chasing a decline just as it does by buying into a sharp rally. Always follow these rules.

1. Wait for a bounce before considering selling short.

2. Never place a *market order* into a rapid advance or decline.

During a rapid advance or decline, a momentum shift in the other direction can occur at any time and without warning. A market order will get filled and if a rapid change in direction occurs, the trade can immediately turn into a major loss.

So always be patient and plan your trades.

How I traded the 2007-2008 decline

This is what happened to me. When I was trading this market in late 2007, I went short with put options on both the SPY and the QQQ (NASDAQ) when the SPY was at $148 after breaking the 200 DMA in early November, right after the first lower high.

See Figure 18d-1 following.

Trading the Trends 215

Figure 18d -1

I used the previous little bounce (minor trend) up to $152 as resistance and my stop for an exit. A close above $152 and I would be out and re-think and re-analyze. About 30 days later the stock traded back up to $152 but never closed above it. And with the options, I used an alert in the event there was an advance, so I was watching it closely. Yes, I was in short very early. Yes, I was very fortunate it did not trade above the $152 and cause me to sell, only to drop again the next day. Here was my thinking.

The highest high was made on low volume, there was higher volume on the ensuing decline, then low volume when making the first lower high.

Then came the breaking of the trend line and the 200 DMA, so I felt the odds were in my favor and was willing to short early. The 200 DMA is a powerful support and resistance level, and I waited for the stock to try to trade back above it. No, not every trade works as well as that one did. But the key to success is always applying the risk versus reward to every decision. Only enter when there is low risk and high reward.

If I had been stopped out, I would simply have waited for the next opportunity, a bounce, so I could short again. When the market is giving signs of weakness and breaking below support levels, listen to what it's saying. Obviously the selling pressure has increased. And at a market top, there is going to be more selling pressure than during a move higher within the channel during the early stages of the public participation phase.

Whether the market is in a long-term uptrend, sideways trend, or downtrend, following any advance the point of least resistance is down. When a stock reaches the upper channel line, many times it is in over-bought territory. And at that particular time advancing further would only increase the odds of a decline. The higher it goes the more selling pressure it finds. So even in a bull market when stocks are advancing, there is a point when more and more investors begin to think, "This is a good time to take my profit."

Yes, I used put options as a means to short the market. And speaking of options, let's learn how to use them safely and effectively.

Chapter 18

The Options Experience

Options are likely the most misunderstood form of trading. The only thing worse in the misunderstood department might be the Forex. There are harrowing nightmarish stories about losing your shirt in options. There are pundits who also claim, "The only people who make money in options are the sellers." So for the conservative perma-bulls, I will show you how to make money as a seller while holding on to your stock. Again, just hang on, we will get there!

All of these negative statements about losing money in options can be true, if you don't know what you're doing. But that is also the case with stocks or any other security, right? I know, some will say, "If you buy a stock and the price drops you still own the stock." Well, that is true. But the folks who didn't know what they were doing and bought dot com stocks that eventually went belly up still lost their money.

Sure, they have a worthless stock certificate, so they can take it and add a few bucks and they can get a cup of coffee. If they add another dollar or two they might get a donut as well.

In the list of stock-owning money-losers, I should probably also include the investors who bought companies like Microsoft, Intel, JDS Uniphase, and Sun Microsystems, to name a few, at their highs in 1999 and 2000.

Intel and Microsoft eventually declined by 50% or more, Sun Micro went to nearly nothing, as did JDSU. Those investors still lost their money.

The point is, whatever you invest in, if you don't know what you are doing, you are likely going to lose money. Whether it's stocks, real estate, options, Forex, or your brother-in-law's new business enterprise he dreamed up last night over a couple of cold beers.

Let's first understand options, and then I'll tell you why people lose money in them. I will also show you how you can trade options safely.

Options can be traded in many ways and for many purposes. One trader might trade options because he doesn't have the funds to trade stocks. Another might trade options because of the leverage an option provides by giving the trader control over a large amount of stock for a small price. Another trader might use options as a protection strategy for his/her investments during a market decline. And another trader may trade options because of the limited risk involved. Meaning, when buying an option, you know the maximum amount you can lose, even if you lose it all.

Regardless of the reasons you may have to trade options, they are a way to make money. They are not simply 'bets' as some call them, but they can be. It all depends on how they are used and for what purpose. In case you do not understand options, let me explain them in their simplest form.

What are Options

There are two basic **types** of options: **Calls and Puts**.

- Buying **Calls** is a long position. These options give you the right to purchase the stock at the strike price of the option until the option expires.

- Buying **Puts** is a short position. These options give you the right to sell the stock at the strike price of the option until the option expires.

Let's make sure you understand the concepts of calls and puts by using a couple of analogies. If you are in possession of a pizza coupon, then you have an 'option.' You are "long" the coupon and have the right, but not the obligation, to buy one pizza for a fixed price over a given time period. In the real world, you do not buy pizza coupons; they are handed out for free. But that doesn't put an end to our analogy because the basic idea is still the same. Possessing a coupon would be the same as if you had purchased a Call Option on a stock or index fund.

Since you are holding the coupon, that means you possess the right to use it, and that's the role of the *Long* position in an Option. Just like buying a call option on the SPY with a strike price of $90 per share. You would have the right, but not the obligation, to exercise that long call and have the stock delivered to you until the option expires.

The pizza storeowner would be *"Short"* the coupon and has an *obligation* to sell you the pizza for the price listed on the coupon in the event you choose to use your coupon.

In the same scenario, whoever sold you the Call Option on SPY has the obligation to sell you the stock at the price listed on the option until the option expires.

You have the right; the seller has the obligation.

If you buy an auto insurance policy you are "Long" the policy, you have paid the premium, and have the right to "Put" your car back to the insurance company. The insurance company is "Short" the policy; it receives money (the premium) in exchange for the potential obligation of having to buy your car from you. Whether you make a claim or not, the insurance company keeps your premium just as the seller of an option would, and just as you would if you *sold an option*. That's the insurance company's compensation for accepting the risk, the premium.

In the real world of car insurance, you cannot just force the insurance company to buy the car back for any reason, and there is not a strike price (set amount) they would have to pay you.

However, in the real world of Put Options, you *can* sell your stock at the fixed price, which is the strike price on the option, for *any* reason while your Put Option is still in effect. There are no restrictions.

The main point is that if you are long, (*buy a put option*), you call the shots. You have the rights. You have the *option* to decide. You have the right to sell your stock for that fixed price at any time during the time your option contract is in effect.

Most option contracts are opened and closed in the open market without a single share of stock ever changing hands. Even though you're allowed to purchase or sell stock with your options, most people never do. Instead, they just buy and sell the option contracts in the open market amongst other traders.

This is because the option price, its value, fluctuates with the price of the underlying stock. So if you buy a Call Option on SPY with a strike price of $90 per share and SPY increases in price on the market, then the value of your option will also increase. Your option is more valuable because you have the right to buy SPY for less than it is selling for on the market. So there is no need to have the stock delivered to you because you can just sell the option you are holding and make the profit.

If you buy a Put Option on SPY with a strike price of $90 per share then you have the right to sell SPY for $90 per share regardless what it is selling for on the market.

If the price of SPY declines, then the value of your Put Option increases because you have the right to sell SPY at a higher price than it is currently selling for on the market. So just like the insurance company, the trader who sold you that call or put option and collected the premium has the obligation. If he sold you a call option and the price of the stock increases, he will lose money. If he sold you a put option and the stock price declines, he will lose money

Options Pricing

An option's price is based on several factors, such as the value of the underlying stock, the length of the option, and the underlying stock's volatility. Stocks that have a history of short-term large-price fluctuation have higher option premiums.

But first, you must understand the expiration and how that affects the current option price. For instance, if the SPY is currently selling for $90 per share on the market and you buy a call option giving you the right to buy SPY for $95 per share, and this option expires worthless in 30 days, then the option price is likely to be very cheap. In trader lingo this is also known as a 'lottery ticket' because the chances are slim that market price of SPY would advance that much within that period of time.

Trading the Trends

Options are a contract. So when you buy either a Call or Put Option, you are buying a contract, and like most contracts, option contracts expire. For instance, for U.S. exchange-listed equity option contracts, the expiration date is on the Saturday that follows the third Friday of the month. And as you know, the market is closed on Saturday, so in reality the option contracts expire on the third Friday of the month. Unless that Friday is a market holiday, in which case the expiration is on the third Friday of the month, and that Friday being a market holiday, the market would be closed. So on those occasions the expiration would be on Thursday.

During the term of the option contract, its value declines the closer it gets to expiration. This is known as *time decay*. This is also something to keep in mind when buying and selling options, but we will address that later. But this time decay is like a curve.

For instance, depending on the expiration of the option the time decay is not severe at the time of purchase. But let's take a 30 day option as an example. The time decay slowly eats away at the value for about 20 days and then the last 10 days before expiration, the time decay drops the value significantly. This time factor can work in your favor as a seller, or against you as a buyer.

As a contract, one option controls 100 shares of stock. So when viewing an options chain that lists all the available options, the bid and ask prices shown must be multiplied by 100. Let's look a typical options chain listing the available call options.

See Figure 19 below.

POWERSHARES QQQ

Symbol	Bid	Ask			
QQQ	51.92	51.93	51.93	-0.35	-0.67

Bid/Ask Underlying security

Calls and Puts | Learn more

⊞ QQQ Aug 26 2011	2 Days to Expiration (Weeklys)
⊞ QQQ Sep 17 2011	24 Days to Expiration
⊟ QQQ Sep 30 2011	37 Days to Expiration

Expire

Calls	Bid	Ask	Last	Change	Vol	Op Int	Strike
49.0 Call	4.05	4.11	4.33	0.18	1	1,249	49.00
50.0 Call	3.35	3.37	3.28	-0.13	225	12,065	50.00
51.0 Call	2.67	2.69	2.66	-0.09	87	1,825	51.00
52.0 Call	2.05	2.07	1.98	-0.16	1,023	2,845	52.00
53.0 Call	1.51	1.53	1.46	-0.11	399	10,870	53.00
54.0 Call	1.06	1.08	1.07	-0.03	474	10,012	54.00

Color Indicates options that are in-the-money   Indicates non-standard option

| ⊟ QQQ Oct 22 2011 | 59 Days to Expiration |

Calls	Bid	Ask	Last	Change	Vol	Op Int	Strike
49.0 Call	4.49	4.50	4.41	-0.19	945	2,115	49.00
50.0 Call	3.78	3.79	3.69	-0.19	1,465	19,658	50.00
51.0 Call	3.11	3.13	3.12	-0.14	927	4,735	51.00
52.0 Call	2.50	2.52	2.41	-0.16	851	8,249	52.00
53.0 Call	1.96	1.97	1.94	-0.06	2,587	11,462	53.00
54.0 Call	1.48	1.49	1.49	-0.04	1,085	16,889	54.00

Figure 19

The above option chain is for the call options on QQQ (NASDAQ). Showing, are the options available that expire September 30, and October 22. As of the date of this options chain, the September options will expire in 37 days and the October options will expire in 59 days.

At the top you will notice the current bid and ask price for the QQQ as it currently trades on the NASDAQ. As its price fluctuates, so do the prices of the options. The QQQ is currently trading at $51.93 per share, and the closest option to that price is the $52 call option that expires in September. It is priced at $2.05, or $205.00. (2.05 X 100 shares = $205)

Thus, for $205 you could control 100 shares of QQQ, $5193 worth of stock, for 37 days until the option expires.

Notice the same $52 call option that doesn't expire until October is selling for $2.50, or $250. You are paying extra for the extra time value. So for $250 you could control 100 shares of QQQ until the October expiration date, or 59 days from the date this option chain was produced.

Now, if you thought the market, and specifically the QQQ, was going to advance within the next 30 days, then buying one of these call options would be a very inexpensive way to make money. It is virtually the same as owning the stock, but with much less capital at risk. The limited risk involved is another reason to trade options. When you buy an option contract, you know going into the trade exactly what you stand to lose in the event you are wrong. You do not have to lose the entire amount of your purchase, but we will discuss that later as well.

By looking at the preceding options chain realizing the current price of QQQ is $51.93 per share, you can see that in order to buy the option, or the right, to purchase that stock for $50 or $49 per share, you must pay more for those options. A Call Option that is less than the current market price of the stock is an "In the Money" option.

Trading the Trends 226

The call options above the current price are "Out of the Money" options. And the further you get out of the money, and\or the closer you get to the expiration date, the cheaper the option price becomes.

Take a look at how the option price fluctuates with the underlying stock. See Figure 19-1 below.

POWERSHARES QQQ TRUST UNIT SER 1

Symbol	Bid	Ask	Last	Change	Change %	B/A Size	High	
QQQ	51.92	51.93	51.93	-0.35	-0.67			

Calls	Bid	Ask	Last	Change	Vol	Op Int	Strike
49.0 Call	4.05	4.11	4.33	0.18	1	1,249	49.00
50.0 Call	3.35	3.37	3.28	-0.13	225	12,065	50.00
51.0 Call	2.67	2.69	2.66	-0.09	87	1,825	51.00
52.0 Call	2.05	2.07	1.98	-0.16	1,023	2,845	52.00
53.0 Call	1.51	1.53	1.46	-0.11	399	10,870	53.00
54.0 Call	1.06	1.08	1.07	-0.03	474	10,012	54.00

POWERSHARES QQQ TRUST UNIT SER 1

Symbol	Bid	Ask	Last	Change	Change %	B/A Size	High	Low
QQQ	52.23	52.33	52.69	0.41	0.78	2000X200	52.42	52.21

Calls	Bid	Ask	Last	Change	Vol	Op Int	Strike
50.0 Call	3.74	3.79	3.85	0.11	0	12,065	50.00
51.0 Call	3.01	3.06	3.06	0.01	0	1,825	51.00
52.0 Call	2.35	2.39	2.40	0.05	0	2,845	52.00
53.0 Call	1.78	1.80	1.80	0.11	0	10,870	53.00
54.0 Call	1.27	1.29	1.30	0.09	0	10,012	54.00
55.0 Call	0.86	0.88	0.88	0.00	0	6,003	55.00

Figure 19-1

Trading the Trends 227

The above option chains were on the same trading day. At the top, the QQQ was trading at $51.93 and the $52 call option was $2.05. At the bottom, the QQQ had advanced to $52.33 and the same call option also advanced to $2.35. The stock advanced $.0.40 and the option value advanced $0.30.

Now let's look at the options chain for Put Options. See Figure 19a below.

POWERSHARES QQQ	Bid/Ask Underlying security					
Symbol	Bid	Ask	Last	Change	Change %	B/A Size	High
QQQ	51.92	51.93	51.93	-0.35	-0.67		

Calls and Puts | Learn more

⊞ QQQ Aug 26 2011		2 Days to Expiration (Weeklys)				Expire	
⊞ QQQ Sep 17 2011		24 Days to Expiration					
⊟ QQQ Sep 30 2011		37 Days to Expiration					
Puts	Bid	Ask	Last	Change	Vol	Op Int	
49.0 Put	1.28	1.29	1.05	-0.11	25	7,246	
50.0 Put	1.54	1.56	1.56	0.17	344	7,340	
51.0 Put	1.86	1.88	1.91	0.20	321	5,582	
52.0 Put	2.25	2.27	2.31	0.23	692	14,009	
53.0 Put	2.71	2.74	2.60	0.06	37	3,878	
54.0 Put	3.26	3.29	3.18	0.12	96	5,323	
⊟ QQQ Oct 22 2011		58 Days to Expiration				Collapse	
Puts	Bid	Ask	Last	Change	Vol	Op Int	
49.0 Put	1.70	1.71	1.76	0.23	10,415	15,698	
50.0 Put	1.99	2.00	2.03	0.20	1,026	44,763	
51.0 Put	2.33	2.34	2.35	0.20	725	12,471	
52.0 Put	2.71	2.73	2.73	0.24	801	64,150	
53.0 Put	3.17	3.18	3.17	0.19	444	14,489	
54.0 Put	3.69	3.70	3.70	0.27	532	9,508	

Figure 19a

The above picture shows the Put Options for the same QQQ as it is trading on the market at $51.93 per share. If you believed the market and/or the QQQ were going to decline in the next 30 days you could buy a Put Option as a means to short the stock. For $225 you could buy the option contract to *Put* the stock to the seller of the option at $52 per share.

As you can see, for a Put Option, the further you get below the current market price of the underlying stock and the shorter the option contract time, the cheaper the option. Also, the further above the current price and longer the time of the option contract, the higher the option price becomes.

In the preceding pictures, I have included the 'in-the-money' and the 'near-the-money' options. These are the most actively traded. However, for some investors the long-term options are more appealing.

Long Term Options

The preceding examples were for the short-term options, but the long-term investor and trader would normally want more time to allow the market to move, especially in a long-term bull or bear market. Long-term options are called Leaps, and have expiration dates from a few months to several years. These are very advantageous when purchased at or near the beginning of a bear market or at the start of a new bull market.

Buying long-term put options at the beginning of a bear market would see the option value increase as the stock value declined. And buying call options at the beginning of a new bull market would see the option value increase as the stock value increased.

Trading the Trends 229

This is a way to invest using less investment capital while still making money during longer term advances and declines in the market. The following picture shows the available options with an expiration date 149 days away. And since the date of expiration has been extended, the option prices increase. See Figure 19b below.

POWERSHARES QQQ TRUST UNIT SER 1

Symbol	Bid	Ask	Last	Change	Change %	B...	...igh
QQQ	51.92	51.93	51.93	-0.35	-0.67		

Calls and Puts | Learn more

QQQ Jan 21 2012   149 Days to Expiration

Calls	Bid	Ask	Last	Change	Vol	Op Int	Strike
50.0 Call	5.18	5.37	5.26	0.09	0	23,758	50.00
51.0 Call	4.60	4.70	4.55	0.00	0	378	51.00
52.0 Call	3.99	4.10	4.10	0.11	0	6,392	52.00
53.0 Call	3.41	3.53	3.14	-0.25	0	1,430	53.00
54.0 Call	2.89	2.98	2.93	0.00	0	2,791	54.00
55.0 Call	2.40	2.50	2.48	0.03	0	36,465	55.00

Puts	Bid	Ask	Last	Change	Vol	Op Int	Strike
50.0 Put	2.97	3.08	3.05	-0.12	0	50,530	50.00
51.0 Put	3.31	3.44	3.38	0.00	0	3,271	51.00
52.0 Put	3.70	3.80	3.81	0.01	0	12,716	52.00
53.0 Put	4.12	4.23	4.56	0.29	0	14,598	53.00
54.0 Put	4.59	4.70	5.10	0.35	0	7,183	54.00
55.0 Put	5.10	5.25	5.11	0.00	0	52,650	55.00

Figure 19b

Yet, an investor could invest in the market without owning the stock. For instance, the QQQ is trading at $51.93 per share. Buying 100 shares of the QQQ would require a $5193 investment. But the $52 call option is priced at $3.99 to $4.10. So, depending on the final trade price when

©Copyright McAllen Publishing

purchasing the option, an investor could control the same 100 shares of QQQ for nearly 5 months for roughly $400. Take a look at the longer term options. See Figure 19c below.

POWERSHARES QQQ TRUST UNIT SER 1

Symbol	Bid	Ask	Last	Change	Change %	B/A Size	High
QQQ	51.92	51.93	51.93	-0.35	-0.67		

Calls and Puts | Learn more

QQQ Jan 19 2013   513 Days to Expiration

Calls	Bid	Ask	Last	Change	Vol	Op Int	Strike
50.0 Call	7.60	7.93	7.60	0.02	0	5,963	50.00
51.0 Call	7.02	7.36	6.90	-0.27	0	593	51.00
52.0 Call	6.47	6.79	6.57	0.00	0	1,589	52.00
53.0 Call	5.94	6.25	6.26	0.32	0	5,797	53.00
54.0 Call	5.45	5.75	5.18	-0.42	0	1,574	54.00
55.0 Call	4.97	5.28	4.75	-0.38	0	10,310	55.00

Puts	Bid	Ask	Last	Change	Vol	Op Int	Strike
50.0 Put	5.90	6.04	6.15	-0.09	0	12,470	50.00
51.0 Put	6.31	6.64	7.69	1.28	0	838	51.00
52.0 Put	6.75	7.09	7.00	0.16	0	1,047	52.00
53.0 Put	7.20	7.57	7.80	0.44	0	4,475	53.00
54.0 Put	7.69	8.06	8.62	0.73	0	1,513	54.00
55.0 Put	8.19	8.58	8.62	0.00	0	5,673	55.00

Figure 19c

Once again, when the expiration is extended, the price increases.

But keep in mind; the prices of the options fluctuate with the underlying stock. And that same options investor could control 100 shares of QQQ for nearly a year and a half (513 days) by buying the $52 call option for about $650.

Trading the Trends

Yes, the price of the option fluctuates along with the underlying stock, and the investor could sell the option at any time for a gain or a loss just like owning the stock.

Generally, the long-term option value is not going to fluctuate as much as the stock. Additionally it will normally not fluctuate as much as the value on the shorter term options.

This is because the minor price fluctuations have time to correct before the long term options expire. So there is less fluctuation with them.

However, this becomes somewhat immaterial when you are looking at the longer-term prospects of profiting in a bear or bull market. The primary trend may continue for more than a year, thus allowing time to obtain sizable gains from the option. For instance, the average bear market declines for 1.7 years. Therefore, buying a long-term put option at the beginning of a bear market could be a very profitable investment.

> I am more and more impressed with the possibilities of history's repeating itself on many different counts. You don't get very far in Wall Street with the simple, convenient conclusion that a given level of prices is not too high.
> ~Benjamin Graham

Chapter 19

The Power of Options

Some have a negative view of options, thinking they are a 'get rich quick' scheme, or possibly may think they are a sure-fire way to 'lose your shirt.' Well, when used properly, they are neither.

As we have seen in the above examples, options are very powerful because of the leverage they provide. The ability to control 100 shares of stock per single option contract for a specified number of days is alluring. Equally alluring is the ability to make huge returns on small investments.

But as always, "If it sounds too good to be true, it probably is." That's why logical and rational decisions must be used in trading options just like trading stocks. Putting money at risk can be done only after calculating the risk and making an informed, strategic decision. Basing a trade decision on some news story or just a *hope* the stock will advance is a loser's strategy.

And we have to keep in mind, even though the option's price is based on the underlying stock, that does not mean the option's price will advance or decline dollar for dollar along

Trading the Trends 233

with the underlying stock price. Let's look at an example and then put the numbers to it. See Figure 19d below.

POWERSHARES QQQ TRUST UNIT SER 1

Symbol	Bid	Ask	Last	Change	Change %
QQQ	51.92	51.93	51.93	-0.35	-0.67

Calls	Bid	Ask	Last	Change	Vol	Op Int	Strike
49.0 Call	4.05	4.11	4.33	0.18	1	1,249	49.00
50.0 Call	3.35	3.37	3.28	-0.13	225	12,065	50.00
51.0 Call	2.67	2.69	2.66	-0.09	87	1,825	51.00
52.0 Call	2.05	2.07	1.98	-0.16	1,023	2,845	52.00
53.0 Call	1.51	1.53	1.46	-0.11	399	10,870	53.00
54.0 Call	1.06	1.08	1.07	-0.03	474	10,012	54.00

POWERSHARES QQQ TRUST UNIT SER 1

Symbol	Bid	Ask	Last	Change	Change %
QQQ	53.15	53.26	53.13	1.30	2.45

Calls	Bid	Ask	Last	Change	Vol	Op Int	Strike
51.0 Call	3.32	3.50	3.32	0.68	1,028	1,625	51.00
52.0 Call	2.69	2.75	2.64	0.54	1,748	2,980	52.00
53.0 Call	2.04	2.09	1.95	0.36	2,469	10,781	53.00
54.0 Call	1.47	1.50	1.49	0.34	1,404	10,376	54.00
55.0 Call	1.01	1.04	0.98	0.20	1,201	6,702	55.00
56.0 Call	0.64	0.67	0.62	0.12	486	5,298	56.00

Figure 19d

The above picture is a good example of how the price of the option tracks the underlying stock's price. At the top of the picture the QQQ was trading at $51.92 per share and the $52 call option was trading at $2.05.

Later that same day, the QQQ had advanced to $53.15 and the $52 call option advanced to $2.69. So as the stock advanced $1.23 per share, the option advanced $0.64. On the surface that probably looks discouraging, but let's look at the numbers.

Buying 100 shares of QQQ stock at $51.92 would require an investment of $5192. Then it advanced to $53.15, or $1.23 per share, for a total of $123 profit.

Buying one $52 call option for $2.05, or $205, would have realized a $0.64 profit while advancing to $2.69, or $269 for a total profit of $64.

That translates into a:

- 31% return on investment for the option
- 2% return on investment for the stock

I know… it looks very tempting to start trading options when you see how cheap they are compared to the price of the stocks and the potentially high return of the options. For instance, you would pay $5192 for 100 shares of stock, yet you could buy a $52 call option on the same 100 shares of stock with expiration 513 days away for only $647. And to think you could invest in a shorter term option for less than three hundred bucks, that is alluring indeed.

But let's not get carried away. People do lose money trading options, so let's understand *why* they lose.

Options Losers

First off, let's eliminate the **lottery ticket** buyers from our discussion. These are the ones who buy far-and-away 'out of the money' options in hopes of a miracle. For instance, in the preceding options chain where the QQQ was trading at $51.93 per share, a lottery ticket buyer may buy a $58 Call Option in hopes the price would skyrocket overnight or at least within the next 30 days. The following picture shows some of the out-of-the-money call options that expire in 37 days. See Figure 19e below.

POWERSHARES QQQ TRUST UNIT SER 1								
Symbol	Bid	Ask	Last	Change	Change %			
QQQ	51.92	51.93	51.93	-0.35	-0.67			
Calls		Bid	Ask	Last	Change	Vol	Op Int	Strike
57.0 Call		0.37	0.39	0.36	0.04	1,975	13,510	57.00
58.0 Call		0.19	0.21	0.20	0.04	64	28,745	58.00
59.0 Call		0.09	0.10	0.08	0.00	4	4,051	59.00
60.0 Call		0.04	0.05	0.04	0.00	4	2,936	60.00

Figure 19e

Yes, a lottery ticket buyer might buy a $58 call option for $0.19 to $0.21 hoping the stock will skyrocket overnight and the option would then be worth something. Another example of a lottery buyer would be buying a put option with a strike price of $44 for nothing more than some pocket change hoping for a market crash.

And yes, the sellers of those type options *are* the only ones who make money on them. And of course the brokerage house gets their commission, we can't leave them out.

Trading the Trends 236

If you are silly enough to buy options that are significantly out of the money hoping for miracles and profit, then you have no business trading options and deserve to lose your money. Go play the lottery; you'll have about the same odds of success.

But for now, let's get back to the *real* traders and investors.

There are some investors who are wise to buy out-of-the-money options, but we'll cover that a little later.

Most people who lose money in options do so because they simply don't know how to trade them. You see, even if the price of the underlying stock does not move, stays exactly the same price as it was the day you purchased your option, the value of your option declines a little each day as it gets closer to expiration. This is called *time decay*.

So some investors lose money in options because they hold the option to expiration while it continues to decline in value. If the price of the underlying stock did not move as expected, the option expires worthless. But if you purchased that $52 QQQ Put Option in the preceding picture and the QQQ actually advanced instead of declined as you expected, then sure, the price of your option would decline, but it would still be worth something, unless of course you held it to expiration, or continued holding it while the stock was going against you. The same goes for the Call options. If the stock moves against you and declines, the option declines in price, but it still has value unless you continue to hold a losing position. Since options do have an expiration date, they will

©Copyright McAllen Publishing

eventually expire worthless unless the stock moves in your favor.

So you see, it's like trading in stocks. If you bought a dot com stock thinking it was going through the roof, but instead it heads south, it is still worth something unless you hold until it becomes worthless. If you short sell a stock and the price advances, you will lose money unless you get out with a small loss.

The main thing to remember with options is the *time*. This is where some lose money, because they fail to consider the time decay. When buying a stock, as long as it doesn't decline, you can hold it and wait for a future advance.

Although the longer term options do give you extra time, you don't have *unlimited* time with options like you do stocks.

With stocks, you only have to be right on the direction that you anticipate the stock to move. You buy it looking for it to advance sometime in the future. And of course, we always want it to advance sooner rather than later. But with options you have to be right on the *direction* **and** the *time*. So the time factor adds another element to the decision process when planning a trade.

Another reason for losses in options trading is what I call *the extremes*. To explain, with options you must have movement in the stock price. If there is no movement in the stock then there is no movement in the option value. But on one side of the extreme are the stocks that are all over the map. They run up one day, and fall the next. This can be advantageous as long as you are on the right side of the trade. But the more extreme the movement, the more difficult it becomes to be right. And stocks that trade with high price volatility also have high option prices. Thus more money is at risk, and that risk is higher.

On the low side of the extreme, if the stock price hardly ever fluctuates up or down, then there is not enough movement to make a profit on the option. Some stocks are just extremely stable and hardly move. These stocks can be stocks with a very low share price. Many stocks that have a share price under $10 per share do not move that much up or down. Maybe ten or twenty cents one way or the other on a good day, but that's not enough to offset the time decay on the option, pay the commission, and make any profit.

There are other stocks like utilities, or maybe some blue chips, that just don't see much movement. Those are difficult to realize a profit on an options trade as well. However, if you own those types of stocks, being an options seller can be very lucrative. We will get to that in just a bit.

For me, I really don't like heart palpitations or a steady diet of Rolaids and Mylanta. So staying somewhere in the middle of the road is much more comfortable. Thus, I normally stay with the SPY, QQQ, and the DIA. The overall market is normally much easier to predict as a whole as opposed to individual stocks, so it is also easier to be right. And staying on the right side of the market is always wise.

Chapter 20

Trading the Trends with Options

When **Trading the Trends** with options, we must include the time factor in our decision. Granted, we aren't dealing with huge dollars, but still, a loss is a loss. And we always protect our capital. As with any trade, we start with the big picture. The following chart is the QQQ. See Figure 20 below.

Figure 20

The primary trend is in an uptrend and the stock has traded within the channel for more than a year. But currently it has traded down to the trend line and appears to have bounced back up. This could be a good setup since it is close to the trend and the 200 DMA and has about $5 headroom just to get back to the upper channel line. So let's take a closer look. See Figure 20a below.

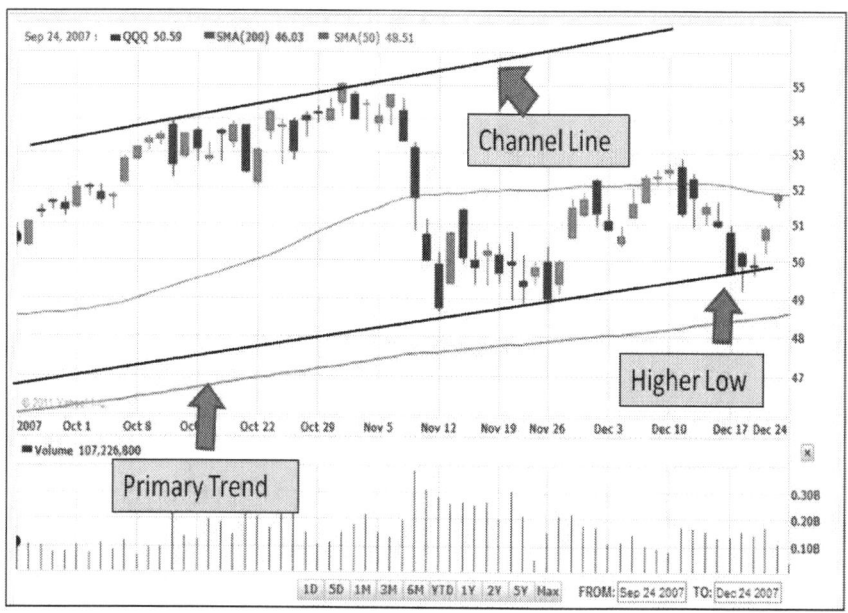

Figure 20a

In analyzing the above chart, there are positives for a trade setup. The stock is trading just below $52 per share, there is minor support at $50, support at $49, and support of the 200 DMA at $48.50. The negatives are the lower high at $53 which will be at least minor resistance and the 50 DMA is just above its head as well.

But let's check the options chain to see what an in-the-money or near-the-money option would cost.

We see the $52 call option is $2.50. See Figure 20b below.

POWERSHARES QQQ TRUST UNIT SER 1								
Symbol	Bid	Ask	Last	Change	Change %	B/A Size	High	
QQQ	51.92	51.93	51.93	-0.35	-0.67			

QQQ Oct 22 2011 — 59 Days to Expiration

Calls	Bid	Ask	Last	Change	Vol	Op Int	Strike
49.0 Call	4.49	4.50	4.41	-0.19	945	2,115	49.00
50.0 Call	3.78	3.79	3.69	-0.19	1,465	19,658	50.00
51.0 Call	3.11	3.13	3.12	-0.14	927	4,735	51.00
52.0 Call	2.50	2.52	2.41	-0.16	851	8,249	52.00
53.0 Call	1.96	1.97	1.94	-0.06	2,587	11,462	53.00
54.0 Call	1.48	1.49	1.49	-0.04	1,085	16,889	54.00

Figure 20b

When considering the time factor of the option, this option will expire in 59 days, but that should be enough time for the stock to trade higher. The stock is trading at $51.93; the $52 call option is less than ten cents out-of-the-money. So with only a small advance in the stock, the option would then be in-the-money. A few-cent rise and changing from being out-of-the-money to in-the-money would really not affect the price of the option that much. But we always want to buy options either close to in-the-money or already in-the-money.

Just to get our feet wet in options, let's buy one $52 call option contract for $250.00 and set an alert at $49 so we can sell it and get out if we are wrong.

Done!

We now control 100 shares of QQQ for the next couple of months. Let's see how our trade went. See Figure 20c below.

Figure 20c

Well, that was a losing trade...

After our purchase, the stock advanced back to the first line of resistance and then tanked. The decline broke the primary trend line and the 200 DMA, not a good sign.

We were in the trade just about two weeks and our option has declined significantly. We might be lucky to have $100 left of our original investment.

What happened? What mistakes did we make?

1. No headroom. We entered at $52 with known resistance $1 away. At the same time, the stock was hitting its head on the 50 DMA, more resistance.

2. Gap. There was an unfilled trading gap the day before our entry and possibly another just below that one.

We were closer to resistance than we were support. Not the ideal entry point.

Besides those obvious mistakes, this is also a case of the market going against you. It happens. Neither the primary trend line nor the 200 DMA provided any support whatsoever. The stock paused one day at the trend line before falling hard. But let's look at the numbers anyway.

If we had bought 1000 shares of the stock at $51.93 per share, or $51,930, and gotten stopped out at $49, we would have had a $2930 loss. If we had bought 10 option contracts for the equivalent of the same 1000 shares of stock at $2500 and lost it all, we would have lost a little less. Losses are painful regardless. But as we have learned, when a stock breaks the trend and the 200 DMA, a true sign of weakness is showing.

Let's analyze again and maybe it's time to switch sides of the market. See Figure 20d following.

Figure 20d

Once our stock broke down, it continued its freefall. We had to wait nearly six months for another safe entry opportunity. We now have a significant lower high, a new declining trend, and our stock is just below the 200 DMA and the new trend line. Since the 200 DMA is no longer advancing and has begun rolling over, that is yet another sign of weakness.

This time, let's place every odd we can in our favor.

Let's take a closer look. See figure 20e following.

Figure 20e

I have extended the new primary upper channel line from the previous high so we can see the stock is already following the channel line lower. We have waited for it to trade up to the declining channel line. At this point we have numerous positives for going short by buying a Put Option.

1. Four lines of resistance. The new trend line, the 200 DMA, the 50 DMA, and resistance at $50 per share that has been tested and failed. All of these sitting right above the stock.

2. There is also a trading gap a few months back at $46 that has yet to be filled.

The only negative on the horizon is a minor support at $47.50 from six days ago that has not yet been tested.

The stock is trading at about $48.00 so we are buying one Put Option contract with a $49 strike price with an expiration of 59 days for $2.75, or $275 dollars. We will set an alert at $50 in the event of an advance and sell our option to close the trade if we are wrong. There is resistance at that level since the stock has traded up to it two times and fallen back. This will hold a loss to a very minimum.

By buying the Put Option with a strike price higher than the stock is currently trading, we are already 'in the money.' Buying this close to resistance allows our alert to be only $1 away from the purchase price. This is also a very low-risk opportunity with four levels of resistance sitting directly above the stock. It really only has two choices. Either muster up the momentum to push through four levels of resistance, or fall.

It is always better to buy 'in the money' options since it places you *squarely* in the trade and raises your chance of higher profit. It also removes all false hopes and any expected miracles. We aren't placing a bet and hoping for a market crash. We are trading, selling short by buying a put option, and doing it only after careful analysis.

It would be a waste of money to buy an out-of-the-money put option with a strike price of say, $42. Sure, it would be cheap. And it might even increase in value a little if the stock dropped by $3 or $4 dollars. But we are also dealing with a time factor. The stock may decline more than that at some point, but maybe not within our option contract term. So any small increase in value of that type option would likely not even cover the commission expense. Buying an option with a

Trading the Trends

strike price that far out-of-the-money simply places most of the odds against the trader.

Buying in-the-money options are like buying or short-selling a stock, you either made the right decision or you didn't. So there is no room to go waffling and change your strategy from a defined and informed decision to some loser's strategy of hanging on to false hopes and praying for miracles.

Options should not be considered bets or gambles. When traded properly, they can be just like trading any other security. Let's see how our trade went this time. See Figure 20f below.

Figure 20f

Within about 45 days from our date of purchase, the stock has dropped about $5 per share from our strike price. I think you can count the money on that one. It looks as though we made our previous loss back and raked in a very nice profit to boot. But we do need to address the risk versus reward for the trade.

The last trade was the purchase of a Put Option with an expiration of just under 60 days. Obviously, it would be time to exit this trade to preserve the gain and to close the trade before expiration.

Now, during every profitable options trade you must always consider the risk versus reward. A good rule of thumb to remember is: **80% of target price.** In our last trade, after falling through the minor support at $47.50 there was no known low the stock might have reached and reversed direction.

But the time in the trade becomes a factor as well. We had a $4 to $5 profit and the risk of losing some of that profit becomes greater than the reward of trying to make an additional fifty cents or a dollar.

And many times there can be a support level the stock might reach and then turn against you taking back some of your profit. So when you have a target price and the stock is within about 80% of that target, it is usually time to exit.

This is because the risk of it turning against you before it actually reaches the target price becomes greater with each move closer to the target. In other words, it's better to sell into the strength as the stock is moving in your direction than to be one of the rats that's trying to get out when it does turn.

This is a strategy I stick to religiously. Sell into the strength, and wait for the rats to start running. When the rats start making their exit, that is what causes the drastic drop in prices. Or in this case after a decline, short sellers start taking profits, traders start buying trying to catch the next bounce, and the bounce may start at any time.

By being out of the trade early, whether it's a buy or a short sale, I am already waiting to flip to the other side before the price has time to turn against me.

Conclusion:

Trading the Trends with options can be very rewarding. But it's important to use the same strategies in the setup of a trade as we did in buying and short selling stocks. You must always have a clear entry and exit point before risking your money. And it does require patience. You have to let the market come to you.

Sure, on our losing options trade, a trader could have flipped immediately and made a lot of money when the stock dropped from $50 to $42 before it finally bounced. But there was no uptrend toward a resistance level, no moving average close by, no known place to put a stop loss, or any means to make an informed decision about a trade and to hold the risk to a bare minimum. So any trade would have been high risk since the stock could have just as easily turned and gone right back up.

Admittedly, in volatile markets when there are no known support or resistance levels, trading options is a safer way to trade. You can manage your money by limiting the number of contracts you buy, and you know exactly what you stand to lose, even if you lose it all. In other words, your loss is limited to the price you paid for the Call or Put Option.

This is not the case with buying stock. With stock, the total price of the stock is at risk on the downside, unless you use a stop loss. And the sky is the limit on a short sale without a Buy Stop.

In other words, if you buy 1000 shares of QQQ for $52 per share, you stand to lose $52,000 without a stop loss. But with options, depending on the option contract you choose, your total loss would be limited to maybe $2000 to $3000.

Traders do lose money in options because there are more ways to lose money in options and they don't factor in all the risks. And too many traders see the small amount of money involved and it is too easy to view the trades as a gamble or a bet. So yes, options can be bets if you use them as such. Options have many uses and can be used for many different purposes.

The Perma-Bulls have been very patient. They have been reading, learning, and waiting their turn. It's time to show them how to protect their bottom line and make money with their investments.

Chapter 21

The Option Protection

Some investors simply can't sell their stock or funds. They are afraid the market will advance in a day or two and they might miss it. They've heard the sales pitches like, "You must stay fully invested so you won't miss the best days in the market." Although, many of these same investors can likely remember some days they wished they weren't in the market at all. But they sit through the declines, the corrections, and the bear markets and wait. Waiting to see more profit at times, and waiting to get back to break even or net-gain territory at other times.

Let me give you some food for thought. If your money was invested in real estate, maybe in a couple of houses down the block you purchased while the real estate market was soft, would you let them sit vacant? Would you just hold them and wait for the real estate values in the neighborhood to go up again?

Probably not. You would want to see some income from those investments. Maybe a rent check coming in the mail every month. At least that would pay for the upkeep, insurance, and the taxes. Your investments in securities are really no different. They also have the ability to produce income without you having to sell at the top and buy back at the bottom.

How can you make money on your investments with options? How can you use options to protect your investments?

First, let's look at how you can protect the bottom line on your investments with options. Then we will see how to use them to generate regular income, just like one of those rent houses.

Remember, you do not need to own the shares of the stock or index fund (SPY, QQQ, or DIA) to buy a Put Option. And options on these indexes are trades on the overall market. By trading the indexes, you don't have to choose a specific stock to make trades on; you can buy Put Options if you think the market is declining or Call Options if you think the market is advancing. So even if you own shares of a mutual fund, you can still use Put Options on the overall market to protect your investment capital.

But if you owned shares of SPY and feared the market was about to head lower, by purchasing a Put Option you have the right to sell your shares for the amount (strike price) of your option contract, the specified price, for a designated period of time (until expiration).

So, in essence, you are purchasing a Put Option at a price near the current market value of your shares for a period of time, and this "insurance" only costs you the amount of the Option. And since options trade for a fraction of the price of the underlying stock, then you are basically "buying insurance." Let's look at the option prices for a stock to get an example. The following table is the option chain for SPY for the options expiring in 36 days.

SPDR S&P 500 ETF TR TR UNIT							
Symbol	Bid	Ask	Last	Change	Change %	B/A Size	
SPY	116.34	116.35	116.28	-1.80	-1.52	3000X3000	
Calls and Puts	Learn more						
SPY Sep 30 2011			36 Days to Expiration				
Strike	Puts	Bid	Ask	Last	Change	Vol	Op Int
80.00	80.0 Put	0.22	0.32	0.30	0.10	6,121	9,100
85.00	85.0 Put	0.35	0.48	0.41	0.07	50	7,500
90.00	90.0 Put	0.55	0.71	0.62	0.14	1,088	12,206
95.00	95.0 Put	0.87	1.03	0.84	0.14	5,172	32,676
96.00	96.0 Put	0.94	1.12	1.05	0.24	8,005	19,238
97.00	97.0 Put	1.02	1.21	0.96	0.10	3	15,396
98.00	98.0 Put	1.13	1.30	1.12	0.24	18	6,751
99.00	99.0 Put	1.24	1.40	1.33	0.29	109	4,467
100.00	100.0 Put	1.34	1.52	1.48	0.36	9,974	30,148
101.00	101.0 Put	1.40	1.64	1.45	0.24	37	23,843
102.00	102.0 Put	1.58	1.76	1.52	0.29	486	11,625
103.00	103.0 Put	1.72	1.90	1.80	0.46	328	4,201
104.00	104.0 Put	1.87	2.05	2.01	0.46	1,024	7,049
105.00	105.0 Put	2.03	2.22	2.16	0.48	10,069	31,378
106.00	106.0 Put	2.16	2.39	2.16	0.35	2,337	4,681
107.00	107.0 Put	2.40	2.58	2.46	0.50	1,346	18,490
108.00	108.0 Put	2.60	2.80	2.45	0.63	1,737	17,759
109.00	109.0 Put	2.81	3.01	2.83	0.49	46,863	20,257
110.00	110.0 Put	3.10	3.26	3.15	0.80	1,938	38,144
111.00	111.0 Put	3.30	3.52	3.60	0.80	1,883	21,085

Figure 21

As you can see at the top, SPY is currently trading on the market at $116.34 per share. Available Put Options start at $80 strike price for $0.32 all the way to the $111 for about $3.50. Look closely at the *option interest (Op Int) and volume (Vol)*.

The volume tells a story here too, just as it does on the charts. Interestingly, the volume on the $80 Put Options is fairly high considering that is so far out of the money. Yet, it tells you there are people who own SPY; they realize a few short years ago it fell below $70 and are worried it could happen again. Possibly even worried it could be worse this time. So for about $0.32 per option contract they are obviously insuring against catastrophe. That volume would also include the lottery ticket buyers hoping for a market crash as well.

The highest volume is on the $109 Puts while the $110 Put volume is very low. This tells you many may think if SPY falls below $110, the risk of it falling farther would be great. And they may be right. So they are insuring against significant decline.

Now, if you owned 100 shares of SPY as an investment and feared the market was headed down and the value in your investment account could fall, you could buy a Put Option to protect your account balance. For instance, if you buy a $105 Put Option at the 'ask price' of $2.03, or $203, then you would have the right to sell 100 shares of SPY at $105 per share at any time from the day of purchase until expiration. Thirty six days to be exact.

So realistically, if you owned 100 shares of SPY and it is currently selling at $116 per share, your investment is actually worth $11600. And for $203 you can guarantee that your investment will not fall below $105 per share for thirty days. If the stock price falls, then you have the option to sell it for $105 per share even if the stock price fell to $0.00. That is 'insurance,' plain and simple.

Does this mean you just threw away $203? No. Your option contract will change in value throughout the day, every day, as the price of the underlying stock fluctuates. It may decrease in value the closer it gets to expiration, but it still has value depending on the current selling price of the underlying stock.

For instance, if the stock price of SPY increases, then your Put Option value will obviously decrease since the market price of the stock is farther away from the strike price of the option. But if the stock price falls in value, then your Put Option value will increase. And obviously, the more the stock price declines, the more valuable your option becomes.

If the stock price fell $10 per share that does not mean you would have to sell your stock for the $105 per share. Instead, you could simply sell your option prior to its expiration for the profit which would offset the decline in the stock price. Thus, you would be protecting the 'bottom line' of your investment account.

Using options as insurance on your investment account does not mean you must own SPY, or any other individual stock. You may own shares of a mutual fund. But you can still insure your investment account by buying Put Options on the overall market, such as options on SPY, QQQ, or DIA. A market decline would cause a decline in your investment account, yet you would be adding profit to your account to offset the decline with the options.

Also note that since the price of the option is based on the current price of the underlying stock, you have other alternatives as well.

For instance: If a week or two passes and the stock price has not fallen, your Option may have decreased in value to let's say $175. At that point you could continue to hold that option, or you could sell it for a small loss and purchase another Put Option for a longer period of time, thus, giving you more time to be protected from a potential decline in your investment. This is simply rolling your option to the next expiration.

Of course, if the price of SPY declined by a few dollars, you might decide to take the profit by selling your option and buying another one with a lower strike price or a later expiration date. These are basic decisions that can be made during the term of the option depending on the market, the economy, and as we say, the *Big Picture*. These decisions take very little effort or time.

The main point is this: You have insurance on your home, your car, your health, and even your life. But do you have insurance on your investments? Your investments are likely your retirement and are certainly a valuable asset. They are no different than your investments in your home or car, and should be protected against loss as well.

Even if you just insured against catastrophe, any insurance would be better than none. Remember, there are no risk-free investments. The financial crisis in 2008 should have been a wake-up call. And no, I am not *Chicken Little*. But this is not *Oz* either. Now I have hopefully gotten your attention. Let's move on.

Options have many uses. Some hold options as insurance on their investments, some trade options for a living exclusively, while others buy them as lottery tickets. But with all of the options changing hands, someone has to be a seller. The market is a Zero Sum Game. For every buyer, there's a seller.

If you are a perma-bull holding stocks that you don't want to sell, then you can make those investments generate regular income just like a rent house. So there is an *option* for you (pun intended).

Selling Call Options

Income Source and Protection

Selling Call Options on stock that you own is what is referred to as selling *'Covered Calls.'* This is a source of income. This is like the pizza store. In our analogy, if the 'Pizza Dude' sold coupons for his pizza, then he would be obligated to honor those coupons at the price listed on the coupon if you held one of his coupons and wanted a pizza at that price. This strategy produces income from your investment while you are holding the investment waiting for it to increase in value. Or it can be used as a *Bearish* approach to protecting the value of your account balance during market declines.

Let me explain. If you fear a decline in the market, as we just learned, you could buy Put Options to protect the value of your account, continue to hold your stock, and make money on the options as the stock price declines.

Thus, you would be offsetting at least a portion of the loss that would have otherwise been a decline in your account balance when the market headed south.

However, there is another way to accomplish this, and can also easily be used to generate income while the stock is not advancing in price, or maybe you feel it may decline.

Selling *Covered Calls*

This strategy can be used at any time as an income generator. Since you already own the stock, buying a Put Option is an expense. However, selling a Covered Call Option is *income!*

The difference is this: If you buy a Put Option, the price of the underlying stock must decline in order for you to make money on your option. Otherwise, the price of the option is an expense or simply insurance for your account balance. But selling a *Covered Call Option* is income to your account. When you sell a Covered Call, you keep the premium you collected for the option regardless. If the price of the stock continues to trade sideways and does not decline, or if it declines, you make money. You *are* the **seller**. And furthermore, as the seller you are counting on the stock price either staying where it is or declining. That way you don't sell your stock, and you make money.

When looking at it from a Bearish perspective, it would be like the pizza store selling coupons that were good for 30 days for one large pepperoni pizza for $10.

If the Pizza Store sold the coupons for $2 each, then the Pizza Dude would make money every time he sold a coupon whether anyone ever used (exercised) a coupon or not.

If the price of pizzas around town declined and could be purchased anywhere for $8 each, then the coupons would be worthless, right? Exactly, but the Pizza Dude still keeps the money from the sale of the coupons.

Let's look at how you would use this strategy in a sideways or declining market. First of all, you would use the same trend lines, channel lines, support, and resistance analysis we have used in every example. When the market is in an advancing primary trend, you would not likely be selling covered calls unless you sold them with a strike price considerably higher than the current price of the stock. And there is certainly nothing wrong with doing that. As you've seen from the option chains, a call option with a strike price much higher than the current market price of the stock is still valuable. They do sell. Traders do buy them.

But in a declining trend, while your account balance would normally be declining with the market, you can profit from selling call options that will most likely never be exercised. They'll expire worthless and you keep the premium paid to you for the option. This is money in your account, and a return on your investment. Just like a rent house bringing in monthly income. Let's look at another option chain.

See Figure 21a below.

SPDR S&P 500 ETF TR TR UNIT

Symbol	Bid	Ask	Last	Change	Change %	B/A Size
SPY	116.29	116.32	116.28	-1.80	-1.52	4000X8

Calls and Puts | Learn more

SPY Sep 30 2011 — 36 Days to Expiration

Calls	Bid	Ask	Last	Change	Vol	Op Int	Strike
114.0 Call	5.92	6.27	6.00	-0.62	236	3,511	114.00
115.0 Call	5.30	5.58	5.38	-0.69	608	3,362	115.00
116.0 Call	4.70	4.93	4.91	-0.31	809	22,004	116.00
117.0 Call	4.10	4.34	4.16	-0.47	2,149	2,688	117.00
118.0 Call	3.60	3.78	3.68	-0.36	2,437	11,194	118.00
119.0 Call	3.10	3.29	3.15	-0.44	640	3,772	119.00

Color Indicates options that are in-the-money   Indicates non-standard option

SPY Oct 22 2011 — 58 Days to Expiration

Calls	Bid	Ask	Last	Change	Vol	Op Int	Strike
114.0 Call	6.84	6.99	6.95	-0.57	3,462	23,805	114.00
115.0 Call	6.20	6.34	6.35	-0.56	10,127	34,320	115.00
116.0 Call	5.59	5.74	5.63	-0.66	9,928	16,693	116.00
117.0 Call	5.01	5.15	5.09	-0.53	13,495	20,223	117.00
118.0 Call	4.45	4.58	4.53	-0.52	9,967	41,617	118.00
119.0 Call	3.92	4.05	4.05	-0.43	8,179	23,562	119.00

Figure 21a

The above picture shows the SPY is currently selling at $116.29 per share. We also see the September options expire in 36 days and the October options expire in 58 Days.

Here's The Setup

Let's say you own 500 shares of SPY, you have analyzed the market with trend and channel lines and believe it would be very unlikely for SPY to advance too much in the next month or so. You might also take into account the time of year, since the market is not known to have too many advances during the summer months. And there may be other economic factors to consider as well.

Or, SPY might even be trading up to, or above, the upper channel line and is due a decline back to the lower trend line. This would generally take a few weeks and might allow time to sell a covered call option and the option expire before the stock traded higher again.

Therefore, you are thinking that either the market is trading sideways, or that SPY's stock price is *not* going to increase before the option expires, and the option will expire in just over 30 days, worthless. By owning 500 shares of SPY, you have the right to sell five covered call option contracts. That way you keep the premium and sell another five option contracts next month doing the same thing again. Rinse and repeat (look at is as monthly income).

Now look at the Call Option '*bid price*' for the **September 119.0 calls for 3.10.** Remember, option price of $3.10 X 100 = $310.00. You own 500 shares, so you can sell five Covered Call option contracts for a total of $1550.

Yes, this means you would be selling a Covered Call Option giving someone the right to buy your 500 shares of SPY stock for $119 per share. You would receive $1550 in your account as the 'premium' for these option contracts. We are assuming you really don't want to sell your stock for whatever reason. Maybe you purchased it at a higher price and need it to advance to just break even. Maybe you originally purchased it at a lower price and simply want to hold it long term. With that in mind, you do have a safety net to prevent someone *calling* the option and forcing you to sell your stock.

Safety Net – Part One

The current price of SPY is $116.29. So you sold the Covered Call Options with a strike price of $119, or about $3 above the current price of the stock. You don't want to lose your stock, so selling above the current price is low risk and this is your first line of safety.

Safety Net – Part Two

Understandably, no one is going to exercise the option and buy your stock unless the stock price increases above $119 per share, because at this time they can buy it cheaper on the open market. But your second line of safety is the ***premium*** they paid to you.

Look at it this way. The buyer of the Option paid $1550 as a premium for the *right* to purchase the 500 shares of stock at $119 per share. That means that since the buyer already paid $3.10 per share for the *right* to buy and this is the premium you keep, then the stock price would have to be above $122.10 (119.00 + 3.10 = 122.10) in order for the buyer to break even on the transaction. Therefore, most likely, this buyer would not 'Call' the option and make you sell unless the price was far enough above $122.10 to be a profitable transaction.

So now, we see the stock would have to advance $6 per share from the current price of $116 to even be a profitable transaction for the buyer of your options to *call the options* and make you sell the stock or force you to buy the options back. And, the stock would have to advance this $6 per share within 30 days before the options expire worthless.

If, and that is a big *if*, the stock price increased enough for the options to be exercised within the next 30 days, then you would be selling your stock for the option price of $119.00 + $3.10 per share collected on the option premium for a total of $122.10 per share. If this happened, that would mean that the price of SPY stock advanced more than $6 per share in a month. Can it happen? Sure, but not likely if the market is weak at the time and you are expecting it to fall. If it does, then you made a profit and can buy the stock back during a pullback or correction. But you do have another alternative.

Safety Net – Part Three

Let's say for instance the price did increase and you did not want to sell your stock. Another alternative would be to simply buy back the options, cancelling out the sale you made. In this scenario, since the price of the stock increased, the value of the $119 options would have increased as well, so you would have a loss on the options sale. But at the same time, since the stock price increased, you would be making a profit on the stock offsetting the loss on the options sale.

By selling out-of-the-money Call Options like we just discussed, you can produce income from your investments during any kind of market. During a declining Bear market, selling Call Options generates income, or you can buy Put Options that will increase in value as the stock prices decline, also adding income to your account. Conversely, during an advancing Bull Market, selling Call Options for prices higher than the current stock price generates income as well.

During a declining market, you could also sell the covered call options on the stock that you own to generate income, and at the same time, be buying put options that would also increase in value during the decline.

These are ways to make money in a sideways or declining market. If you do not own the stock, then the put options are a great alternative.

Many do not understand options and never take advantage of the ways to make money with them. Some think, "Why would someone buy an out-of-the-money option $3 away from the current market price of the stock?" But it doesn't matter *why* someone would do it, they do! Go back and look at the volume in the options chain (Figure 21a). Thousands of contracts sold every day, and the current bid price is right there. All you have to do is offer them for sale at the current bid price. It doesn't get much simpler than that.

You want a guarantee?

Some perma-bulls are so tight they can squeeze the head off of a nickel. And that's fine. Money is hard to come by, and losing it hurts. Some say that those who made money and lost it can make it back faster. The reasoning behind this theory is, they can make it back faster because they now know how to make it. They've already done it once, so they don't have to learn how to do it.

I'm not sure if I agree with that theory or not. It sounds logical. But making money is never easy. So it's always better to keep it than to have to try to make it again!

So if you want a guarantee that you will make money and not lose your stock, then you can have that as well. Let me show you how.

> "Stock market bubbles don't grow out of thin air. They have a solid basis in reality, but reality is distorted by a misconception."
> ~ George Soros

Chapter 22

The Option Spread

Your Guarantee to NOT Lose Money

Are you a scared Perma-Bull? Some simply fear they are wrong in thinking the market will decline, and instead of trading sideways or declining it will go up and they'll lose their 500 shares of stock. They want a guarantee.

Don't worry; you can buy 'Insurance' *even* on your Option!

The Option Spread

Traders who deal in options use many different types of option 'Spreads.' There are Butterfly Spreads, Debit Spreads, Credit Spreads, Straddles, Strangles, and many other variations as well.

But for the individual investor, the investor who fears the market might advance when least expected and the Covered Call Option he/she sold might get 'called' and hand him/her a loss, the most basic type of 'Option Spread' to protect your stock is the **Bear Call Spread**.

©Copyright McAllen Publishing

Trading the Trends

This is actually a Credit Spread option that will generate income, has a very low risk, and will protect your account balance at the same time.

The strategy is to **'Sell a Call' and 'Buy a Call' at the same time**. That may sound utterly ridiculous, but it's not.

No, it's certainly not ridiculous. Let's look at how this strategy works. First, take a look at the option chain for SPY again. This time I have included additional out-of-the-money call options that are further away from the current market price of the stock. See Figure 21a below.

SPDR S&P 500 ETF TR TR UNIT

Symbol	Bid	Ask	Last	Change	Change %	B/A Size
SPY	116.29	116.32	116.28	-1.80	-1.52	4000X8

Calls and Puts | Learn more

SPY Sep 30 2011 — 36 Days to Expiration

Calls	Bid	Ask	Last	Change	Vol	Op Int	Strike
114.0 Call	5.92	6.27	6.00	-0.62	236	3,511	114.00
115.0 Call	5.30	5.58	5.38	-0.69	608	3,362	115.00
116.0 Call	4.70	4.93	4.91	-0.31	809	22,004	116.00
117.0 Call	4.10	4.34	4.16	0.02	0	2,760	117.00
118.0 Call	3.60	3.78	3.68	0.11	0	11,762	118.00
119.0 Call	3.10	3.29	3.15	-0.17	0	4,072	119.00
120.0 Call	2.60	2.79	2.72	0.00	0	14,899	120.00
121.0 Call	2.17	2.37	2.29	-0.08	0	13,556	121.00
122.0 Call	1.77	1.95	1.90	-0.10	0	46,834	122.00
123.0 Call	1.45	1.62	1.55	-0.09	0	5,446	123.00

Figure 21b

Remember, you were selling five Covered Call Options for your 500 shares of SPY at $119 strike price for $3.10 each.

Now look at the Option Chain again just below the 3.10 price for the $119 Call Options. Notice the $122 Call Options are $1.95, and both the $119 and the $122 Call Options expire at the exact same time, on the same day.

This strategy is to buy insurance on the options you sold. So, to cover your sale of Cover Calls, simply buy five of the $122 Options for 1.95. That's right. You sold five Option Contracts at $3.10 and now you are buying five Contracts at $1.95.

Now let's look at the numbers.

- $1550 Income from the sale of five Covered Calls at $3.10 ($310) each.

- $975 Paid to buy five Calls at $1.95 ($195) each.

- $575 Net income in your account.

Now then, what can happen? What are the scenarios?

1. The price of SPY trades sideways for the next 30 days fluctuating very little, and both the $119 and the $122 Option Contracts expire worthless.

Result - You made $575 in 30 days.

2. The price of SPY declines. It doesn't matter how much, because any decline will cause both the $119 and the $122 Call Options to expire worthless.

Result - You still made $575 in 30 days

3. The price of SPY rallies and advances above both option prices, let's say to $126.00 per share, although it doesn't matter how high it goes, because you bought five Call Options for the *right* to purchase SPY at $122.

Result - In this scenario, your maximum loss is *always* the difference in the strike price of the options, less the net income received from the sale and purchase. Therefore, there is $3 difference in the strike prices ($122 – $119) for five contracts equaling $1500 less the $575 net premium you received.

Total Maximum Loss is $925.00

Obviously, in this scenario the investor is doubtful the price would increase, therefore would be comfortable in making the money from collecting the premium from the sale of the options. However, even in this worst case scenario, where the price of SPY advanced unexpectedly from $116.29 to $126.00 per share causing a loss on the option trades of $925, look at the **REAL** bottom line.

Result - You still own your 500 shares of SPY, and would have realized a $10 per share gain in the stock price equal to $5000.

So in reality, there really is no worst-case scenario. If the price of SPY remains the same or declines, you made money on the options, and if SPY advances, you made money on the stock and lost a fraction on the options. Thus, you made money either way.

Thus, in the event SPY advanced to $126, you made $5000 on the stock advance and lost $925 on the options for a total profit of $4075. But you can do better than that.

The No Loss - Limited Loss Strategy

Another advantage to the above strategy is to even limit the loss of the option contracts in the event the stock is advancing in price. This way, you make money on the stock that is advancing, and you do not lose money, or you at least limit the amount you lose on the option trades.

Remember, as the price of the stock advances, both the $119 and the $122 call option contracts are becoming more valuable. In this scenario, as the price of SPY increases, the individual who purchased the five contracts from you would see an increase in value of the call options he is now holding. But you are also holding five contracts that will also increase in value at the same time.

This means you do have the right to buy back your five option contracts for a small loss and sell the five contracts you purchased for a profit at the same time to offset the loss of the contracts you originally sold.

Another alternative would be to buy back the five contracts that you initially sold and continue holding the five contracts that you purchased for a larger profit as the stock price increases. This scenario is allowing you to profit not only on the 500 shares of stock that you own, but also profit on 500 more shares as the option price increases in value.

And, there is yet another alternative to this strategy.

In the event the stock declines as you initially expected, then you also have the right to sell the five contracts you purchased as insurance on your options sale while they have value. This obviously reduces the amount you would lose on those by allowing them to expire worthless.

Conclusion:

Options are not lottery tickets. They can be, for those who buy cheap options for a few pennies that have a strike price (exercise price) considerably higher or lower than the current price of the underlying stock or index fund. These options that are so far out-of-the-money are only worth anything in the event there is a disaster and the underlying stock price falls dramatically or runs up in value, depending on the type of option purchased. Of course, one may also decide to sell these out-of-the-money options on stock currently owned as a source of income, which would obviously be very low risk.

Buying Put Options is a great strategy to protect your capital during a declining market. Selling options can produce steady income while simply holding investments waiting for an advance, especially if you happen to own some 'Widows and Orphans' stock. You know... Stocks in blue chip companies that hardly ever move up or down in price but pay a good dividend.

Selling Call Options is a bearish approach to the market. But after analyzing the market, and/or your stock, using trend analysis and technical analysis, you are able to make very low risk trades to profit in any market environment. This is income for you, plain and simple.

Chapter 23

Trading the Secondary

For some, short-term trading is thought of as nothing but day trading. And of course, day trading has a less than appealing view by most observers. This is simply because there are not many people who become consistently successful as a day trader. And no, I would not recommend day trading as a career for most investors or traders because as I have said, I really don't have a hankering for Rolaids and Mylanta.

But trading the secondary trends can be much less stressful than day trading. With day trading the trader is trying to capture a few pennies on every little price fluctuation during the day. Then counting those pennies to make sure the losses were less than the profits.

Trading the Trends

We've covered how to recognize the trends in a 3-trend market, trade with the primary trend, and stay on the right side of the market.

And for the long-term investor, **Trading the Trends** is critical for success. But only trading the primary trend leaves out a whole segment of potential profit.

As you know, there were times we waited months for the market to come to us, to find a very low risk entry point, and to place a trade. Long waits can wear the patience mighty thin.

But now that we've covered options, we can see the potential for profit in options while risking very little capital. And limited risk with a potential for high return is something most of us are interested in.

But it's never as simple as some try to lead you to believe. We all know the saying, "If it sounds too good to be true, it probably is." And that is one caveat for trading the secondary and minor trends. Regardless of the investment, any time there is potential for high profit, the risk of loss is also high.

But to start, take a look at the following chart of the QQQ. Based on what you see the price movement has been, think about what you would envision the market doing next.

See Figure 22 following.

Figure 22

In using the QQQ we exclude any individual volatility of any one stock. It's much easier to be right on the bigger picture than it is on the little one. I also included the short-term trend and channel lines.

That's pretty easy. Looking at a six-month chart, the stock has already made three highs, and after the first two it fell back to the trend line, which by the way is no longer in an uptrend. So it would appear the next logical move is back down. And likely that might take 30 days to complete if it continues to trade the same as it has in the recent past.

If you said the stock should move lower in the near term, you were right. I extended the chart in time, see Figure 22a following.

Trading the Trends

Figure 22a

It fell from the high of just above $59 per share to $50 per share in a couple weeks' time. This is where trading the secondary and minor trends can also be low-risk and very profitable. The entry point is always the key.

When you look back at the charts of our previous trades, there were many opportunities to enter a short position when the stock traded up to the channel line.

In the event you own the stock for the long term, you can still make money from the minor declines even during an advancing market. Yes, you are trading against the primary trend. But as you know, even the secondary and minor trends within an advancing primary trend can lead to a good profit. This is where the minor trends within the secondary trend work in the trader's favor. Many times the minor trend can be used as a support or resistance level to either enter the trade or get out if the market goes against you. Let's look at a good example of this. See Figure 22b below.

Figure 22b

The above chart has a lot of very useful information for the short-term trader. Let's start with the small arrows indicating the gaps in trading. Remember, gaps are closed more often than not.

On the left side of the chart there are two gaps on the first decline. Both of those were closed within about two weeks on the following advance.

Trading the Trends

The short term trader should notice the gaps, and instead of thinking that gaps are powerful and will add to a decline or advance, think about when they will close.

Notice, after the first low, there was a gap on the next advance that I didn't mark with an arrow.

This is because although there was a definite gap between the close one day and the open the next, the wicks of the candles overlap. This tells us that the trading range those days actually overlapped and many times that is considered as closing the gap. On the second advance a huge gap was opened. It took about 30 days to trade back down to close it.

The point is, on the first decline, a short-term trader would see the gaps and be looking for the stock to find support in order to buy a call option. And after three negative days at the bottom, with the second and third day closing higher, that would indicate temporary support was found. The fourth day was a positive day, trading just above $55 per share and a good place to buy a call option. There is at least minor support $1 lower, there are two open gaps that are likely to be closed, and known resistance is $3 away at the previous high.

By entering the trade with a $55 call option on March 21, the trader could close the trade within two weeks at the first sign of weakness for a better than $2 profit.

This trade is partly anticipatory and partly technical analysis. The trader would not be trying to pick a bottom. He would anticipate the gaps being filled, but wait for the first positive

Trading the Trends

day after the bottom was formed to enter. Then exit with a profit.

Short term trading is not always about waiting for a stock to trade back up to the channel line.

It may never make it. It may head lower at any time. The channel and trend lines are great tools to use. But when trading short term, quick profit is the key because with options you are also trading against time. If you buy an option that expires in 30 or 60 days, then your profit must come soon. Let's look at another trade with the same chart. See Figure 22b below.

Figure 22b

The second trade would be after the higher low. No, there's likely no way a trader could pick that bottom when the higher low was made.

Trading the Trends

The only indicators were the positive trading days after a more than 5-day decline and the candle at the bottom with a long wick (handle) and a small top and has the appearance of a 'hammer'. Those candles appearing after a decline are good indicators of support. And some traders would see that candle form and buy a call option anticipating another advance.

The third trade would be the safer trade. Buy a put option after the advance at the top. That's right, shorting tops instead of buying bottoms. When the stock hit resistance and traded four days, unable to break out, is a good place to buy a put option after the third or fourth day of the stock being unable to advance. Buy the option at the top, anticipating a decline to at least fill the gap, and closing the trade if the stock traded higher. Very low risk, close the trade if the stock breaks out above resistance, and close to $3 profit in the event the stock trades lower just to close the gap.

Yes, buying a put option at the top of an advance is sometimes the best trade. Stocks fall faster than they advance. Thus, your money spends less time in the market, and less time tied to an expiring asset. Whether we like it or not, the market in general goes to the point of least resistance. And an advance is usually against more resistance than a decline, since most traders will sell quicker than they will buy. And of course, the more a stock advances, the greater the resistance becomes. So buying put options at the top of an advance increases the odds of quick profit, being in and out of the trade before the option loses very much value due to time decay.

The long-term options (leaps) do not fluctuate as much as the shorter-term options. Yet you need enough time for the stock to make a move. So either the 30-day or 60-day expirations are usually the ones traders use. I realize a $3 profit sounds small. But when trading options, one option might cost $2 to $3 depending on the stock, strike price, and the expiration chosen. So a $3 profit can be a huge return on your money.

Again, this is higher-risk trading. But the risk can be reduced by using technical analysis, trends, channels, and general market knowledge. It requires patience to wait for the right setup, and defined personal trading rules to exit a trade quickly when it goes against you. Keep the losses small. Analyze every loss and learn from it.

Yes, options are higher risk because you have to be right on both the direction and the time. But with higher risk also comes higher rewards. So the best approach is to use the tools you have to make the best decisions, like waiting for a stock to trade up to resistance. At that point it only has two choices. Either garner the momentum and strength to push through resistance and move higher or decline.

And if you are holding a put option, you are cheering for the decline. And you have put yourself in the best position possible to reap the reward. You've used your tools to find the right entry point at the resistance level, so you are also using the stock's weakness against it.

That is the way to place the odds of success in your favor!

Chapter 24

Growling Bull Strategy

Having the heart of a bull while experiencing some hankering to growl like a bear, hibernate, and scare the bejesus out of unsuspecting hikers is not an uncommon trait. Some might think such an individual should seek professional psychiatric help and spend countless hours lying on a sofa explaining in graphic detail how the market makes them *feel*. But there is actually a trading strategy for those who suffer from this terrible condition.

I call it the Growling Bull Strategy. We don't know what the market will do tomorrow. We don't even know what it will do today. Many times the market opens higher, advances, and then sells off. Other times the market may open flat or lower, sell off, and then rebound to end the day positive. That is one reason we use 3-month charts for our short-term trading decisions. That way we eliminate the noise, use technical analysis to pinpoint possible reversals, and make informed decisions.

We may not know what the market will do today. What we do know is what history has taught us. We know a primary trend continues until something significant proves the trend has changed.

As we traded the up-trends that were consistently range-bound within the channel, many stock investors and traders were sorely tempted to sell at every high and reenter when the stock declined to the lower trend line. But there's a problem with attempting that type of exit and reentry strategy. The exit is easy, just sell at the high; any high will do as long it is profitable. But oftentimes finding a new entry point proves difficult. Especially since there are times while in an advancing primary trend the market is trading above the 200 DMA. So there may be no known support level to create a safe entry point other than the trend line itself.

Yet, during these advancing times, the stock continues to decline by $5 or $10 per share before returning to a new high, usually very close to the upper channel line we drew starting with the first two highs of the trend. Some traders realize this is additional profit that could be made on every decline and subsequent advance. Simply getting out at the top, and reentering after a pullback could drastically increase profits while being on the sidelines during the declines.

The growling bull strategy is for those traders, and possibly some investors, who want to be completely sure that they won't kill off their favorite investment with one bad mouse-click. It would be irritating to be on the sidelines when the stock moved higher instead of declining back to the lower trend line as you expected.

Trading the Trends | 283

The growling bulls sell market tops by buying put options while still holding his/her investments or stock. Thus, the bull captures some profit on all those pullbacks in an advancing market and is already holding a short position in the event any of those pullbacks turn out to be a huge decline. And inevitably, they do. So it's a little insurance and potential profit as well. At the same time, the long-term investments are left intact in the event of further advance.

Let's explore how it works in an advancing market. We'll start with the big picture. See Figure 23 below.

Figure 23

For the short-term trader, the mid-term trader, or the perma-bull, there were many opportunities in the above chart to sell market tops.

By drawing an upper channel line after the first two highs were formed and then adding a lower trend line on subsequent lows, there would have been at least five opportunities over the period of a year to capture a $5 or more profit during the pullbacks.

I won't tell you it's easy, because it's not. But when you look back at all prior market advances and declines, the stair-step picture is always there. That is just how the market moves. Another realization is the fact that anytime the market or an individual stock advances too far, too fast, then the advance is not sustainable.

Meaning, even in the event you were short and the price began a rapid advance, you might lose a little on the put options you were holding, but the opportunity to sell at even a higher unsustainable top by buying more puts would be even more profitable.

Now, the preceding chart shows after the first two highs were formed and the channel line could be drawn, then the opportunities were there to sell three tops. By selling when the stock reached the upper channel line, the trader could have sold one in late August, one in mid-September, and one in mid-October. All three should have been profitable. But then selling another in mid-November would have likely caused a loss.

Before we look at the numbers, let's take a closer look at the mid-November timeframe.

See Figure 23a following.

Trading the Trends   285

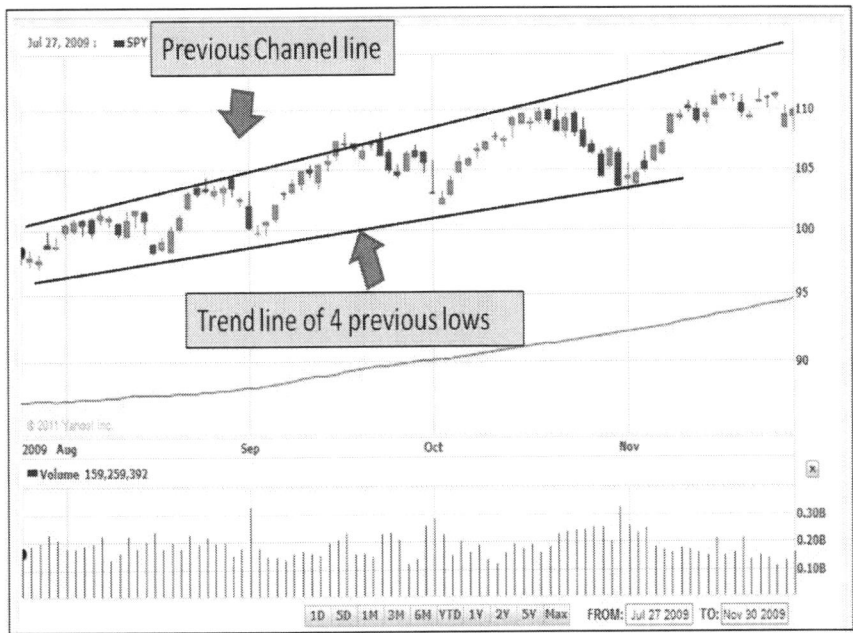

Figure 23a

First of all, a trader who had been selling the tops may have not sold a top in November.

The reason being, the stock was in the middle of the old channel, it had never reached the previous upper channel line. But for the sake of argument, the stock did advance about $7 from the low of $104 to $111. So let's assume the trader decided with that advance it was time for a pullback and bought some put options. So let's check the options chain.

See Figure 23b following.

©Copyright McAllen Publishing

SPDR S&P 500 ETF TR TR UNIT					📉 S&P Options Report			
Symbol	Bid	Ask	Last	Change	Change %	B/A Size		High
SPY								
🔼 Calls and Puts								
104.00	104.0 Put ▶		1.87	2.05	2.01	-0.05	0	7,349
105.00	105.0 Put ▶		2.03	2.22	2.16	0.23	0	34,630
106.00	106.0 Put ▶		2.16	2.39	2.16	0.00	0	6,269
107.00	107.0 Put ▶		2.40	2.58	2.46	0.11	0	18,287
108.00	108.0 Put ▶		2.60	2.80	2.45	-0.12	0	16,147
109.00	109.0 Put ▶		2.81	3.01	2.83	0.00	0	61,717
110.00	110.0 Put ▶		3.10	3.26	3.15	0.05	0	41,952
111.00	111.0 Put ▶		3.30	3.52	3.15	-0.37	0	22,675
112.00	112.0 Put ▶		3.61	3.80	3.72	-0.15	0	85,886

If the trader owned 1000 shares of SPY and it is selling at $110 per share, that's $110,000 value in the investment account. The shares have rallied from $104, and now are at $110 for about a $6000 gain. But for some insurance, we'll just buy three put option contracts at the $109 strike price for 2.81 each for a total of $843. (2.81 X 100 X 3=843)

With this setup, if the stock moves higher, then we will lose some money on the options, but we will make money on the stock. If the stock declines, we will lose money on the stock but make money on the options.

Note: I use the term 'stock' in this example, however, an investor holding mutual funds could also apply this strategy to an investing plan by buying put options on an index like the SPY, QQQ, or the DIA.

Take a look at what happened. See Figure 23c following.

Figure 23c

Buying the put options in mid-November would have resulted in the stock moving sideways for a month while the options decreased in value due to the time decay. By mid-December the options that had been purchased with a 60-day expiration would have about 30 days left until expiration and possibly two-thirds of their original value. The value of the options would hold up better because the stock had not moved in price. But we probably should decide how to proceed. We have a couple of choices.

1. **Continue to hold the options even if they eventually expire worthless. This is bound to happen if the stock advances or continues to trade sideways.**
2. **Sell the options for a small loss and buy some new options with a later expiration date.**

Realistically, we are cheering for the stock to move higher since it is our real investment anyway. Plus, we already made money on put options by buying them at the three previous highs and selling for a profit after the stock traded back to the trend line. But the best choice is to keep the expiration as far in the future as reasonably possible.

So let's take the loss and buy three more contracts that won't expire until the third Friday in February.

As it turned out, the stock did advance another $5 which might have caused the trader to sell the options for another loss and buy more with a higher strike price. Or, the trader might have just held on and waited.

But let's see what happened next. See Figure 23d below.

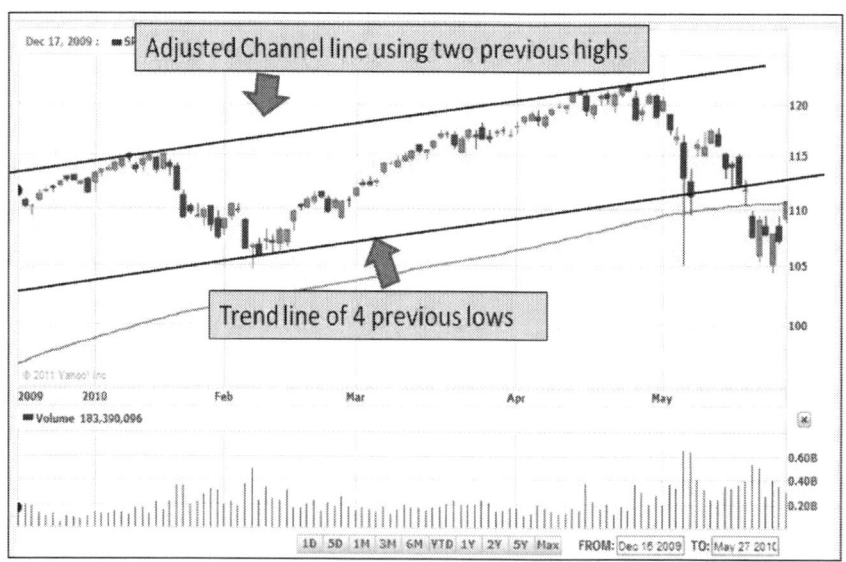

Figure 23d

By mid-February the stock does get a $10 haircut in price. But then advances, setting up another scenario of deciding when to go short. However, the decision would have been made simpler by adjusting the channel line using the last two highs. And once again the options would have paid off in spades when the stock drops more than $15.

In the event the trader lost money two times after buying options and the stock advanced, the $15 decline would have likely healed those wounds. And at the same time, instead of being down $15,000 in the investment account due to the decline in the stock price, a great deal of that loss would have been offset due to the profit on the options.

But we don't want something to be easy. Let's take a stab at a sideways market. Those always present much more of a challenge. See Figure 23e below.

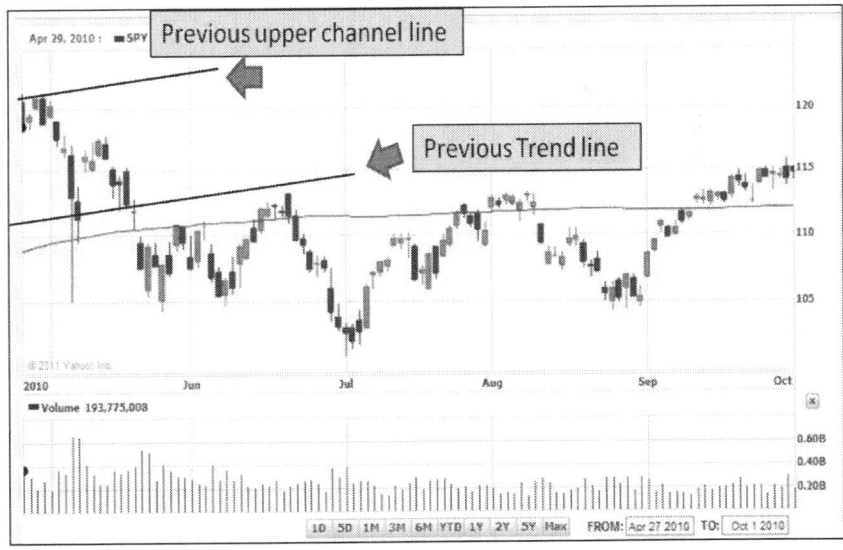

Figure 23e

To keep it simple, I extended the previous chart. The last purchase of put options at the $120 level paid off handsomely. Especially when it looks like the stock *fell out of bed* by trading down about $10 in one day.

On the preceding chart the stock found a temporary bottom in early June before bouncing back up above the 200 DMA to the $112 level. At the top of this bounce, the first day it closed below the 200 DMA would have been an excellent buy point for put options. Look at the setup. This is the type of chart pattern you sit on the sidelines and wait for. This is the market handing you a gift. Let's analyze the perfection as it is a learning experience.

At that point, when the stock traded up to $112, look at the positives.

1. **There is more than 5-day advance**

2. **It is showing the inability to move higher, and is up against major resistance of the 200 DMA.**

3. **It's already proven it is weak from the previous decline.**

4. **Minimum risk. Close the sale if it trades $1 higher.**

5. **The potential for a $5 gain on the options even if the stock only traded back down to the previous level of $105 to test that support.**

It doesn't get much better than that. And obviously many traders felt the same way since the decline resulted in a $10 to $12 drop.

The next bounce may have fooled some. It was another 5-day advance, traded three days at the $110 level, dropped one day and then advanced further. Sure, buying options there would have seen a temporary loss when it advanced to $112 before heading lower again.

But that's the peril of trading a sideways market. And you certainly can't be a winner every time. But in this case, you would rather lose on the options since that would mean your real investment was advancing. At the same time, you want to make sure you protect your bottom line on the investment account. So options become a necessity.

After that first low, the market trends sideways for three months and there is no way of knowing which way it will eventually go. That is the difficulty with a sideways market when trying to figure out when it's time to buy. And many times it is ***not*** a time to buy.

That's why in our earlier trades we waited for the market to move above the 200 DMA and show enough strength to hold support before entering a trade. Because a sideways market may be just as likely to head lower as it is to head higher. And many times after breaking the 200 DMA and the primary trend line, it is *more* likely to head lower. But for the investors who are holding stocks or mutual funds, a little insurance might make for a better night's sleep.

Let's look at one more setup on that same chart.

See Figure 23e below.

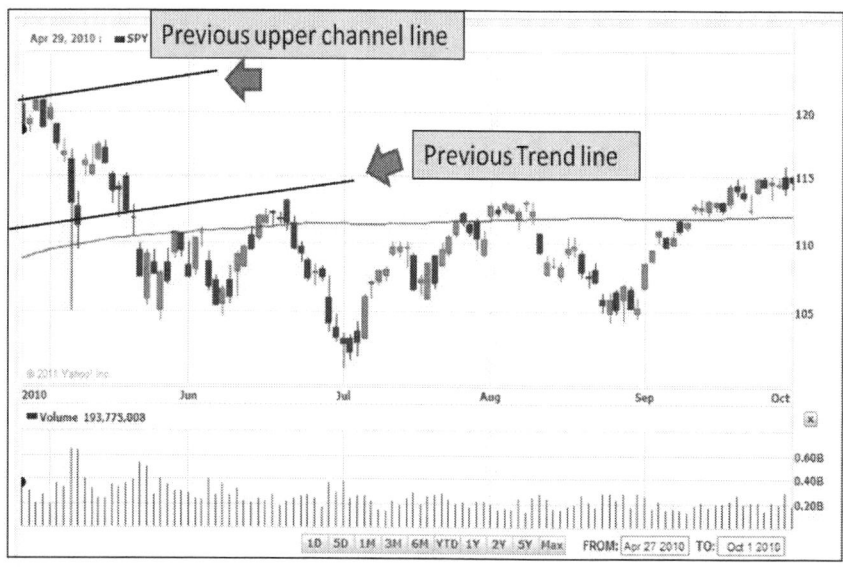

Figure 23e

After the lowest low, history repeated itself. The stock traded right back up to the $112 level and found that same resistance once again. This time it trades about eight days at that level. Yes, we know by the color of the candles it was showing some strength by closing positive each of those days, yet still was not advancing. But it is daring the trader. The day it moved above the 200 DMA it gapped up. There is a gap that may be filled, and that gap just happens to be under the 200 DMA. If it trades lower to fill that gap, then it is back under stiff resistance.

Sorry, but the last time it was at this level it dropped ten bucks. I would be too tempted to take the dare. Buy a put option at the high of one of those trading days, close the sale if it traded $1 higher, and take that chance. That's a $1 risk for a potential $10 reward. I like those odds.

That is the type of trades a trader looks for. The stock banging it's head on resistance and support being a good stretch away.

When short-selling stocks or buying put options, you are *always* selling tops. Regardless if the primary trend is up, down, or sideways, you have to wait for an advance in order to go short. And when buying puts, that way at least the options have a good chance of delivering a profit. And by waiting for an advance, even if the stock advances further, you still made money on it even though you lost a little on the options.

When you think about selling tops or waiting for a bounce to go short, think of a rubber band. In the case of a rubber band, the further you stretch it in one direction, the harder it snaps back once you release it. It's a simple action and reaction, and is nothing more than the tendency to regress to the mean.

Markets are really no different. The further you stretch the stock market the more violent and persistent the snap back tends to be once the turn occurs. And the further a market is stretched away from the mean, the more violent the snap back tends to be once the pressure is released.

It is never a simple matter of buy low and sell high or sell high and buy low. If it were easy, everybody would do it, and they'd all be rich. There will be times when the stock continues to advance and the options will lose money. Then there are other times the options will pay huge rewards, such as on the preceding chart when the stock dropped about $20 per share. Those are the times the Perma-Bull and the Growling Bull are thankful for *insurance* and any previous losses on the options suddenly become insignificant. Let's look at a declining market. See Figure 23f below.

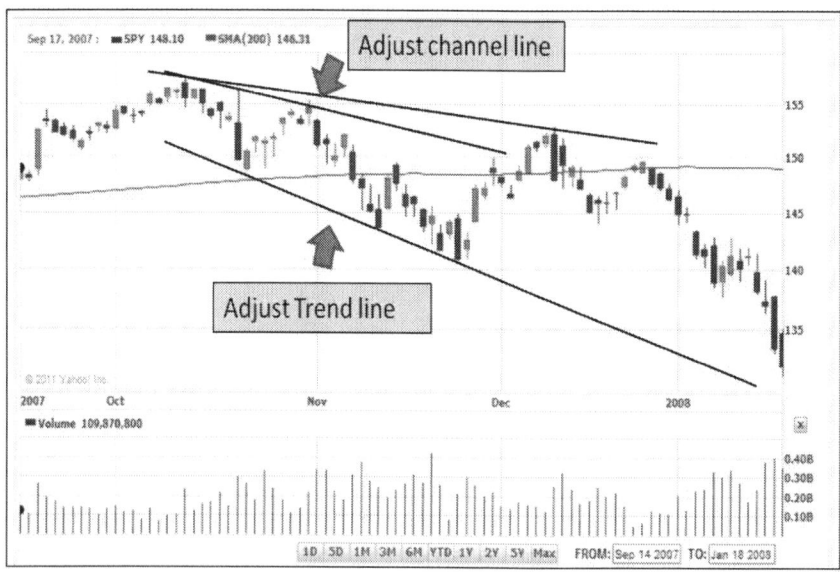

Figure 23f

The above chart shows as soon as the first lower high was formed a channel line could be drawn providing a target for entering a short position. Selling tops is a matter of buying puts *after* an advance whether the market is advancing, declining, or trading sideways. There were numerous entry points in this chart, but again, the best short entries are after at least a five-day advance.

Once the price declines to a certain level the selling pressure eases and a bounce back occurs. Just like a rubber band. In the preceding chart, any entry after a five-day advance would have paid off immensely.

By using the two most recent lows and highs, you can adjust the trend and channel lines to assist in finding entry points in a sideways or declining market. As significant lows and highs form, adjust your primary trend and channel lines accordingly.

The market moves in mysterious ways. It goes up when least expected and drops faster than you can imagine. It always moves higher than anyone might think it should and falls farther than the most astute trader would ever suspect.

No, it's never simple. But we shouldn't make it more difficult than it is, either. It's a matter of calculating the potential loss on options against the potential gain on the stock. For instance, if the stock is trading at $118 per share, an advance of $5 translates into a gain of $5000 if you're holding 1000 shares. If the put options cost $1000 for three contracts, then that will at least insure 33% of your investment from a huge loss, and even if the stock advances and you allow the options to expire worthless, you are still money ahead.

But it doesn't take a rocket scientist to figure that you can be wrong and lose money three times out of four, but the one time you do make money with the options can be a life saver.

And no, it would make no sense to spend more money on options than potential profits on the stock. But at the same time, it makes no sense to be holding uninsured investments.

Personally, I hate paying insurance. But I would rather the health insurance company continue to make money on the premiums than for me to experience the alternative. So I bite the bullet and send them money.

I might be fortunate and continue experiencing good health for years to come while the insurance company pads their pockets. But with investments, there is no doubt there will be a correction or pullback at some point, likely in the near future, and it will take money from your bottom line.

Corrections can, and do, turn into bear markets. And suffering through a bear market watching your investment account balance evaporate into thin air is about as painful as it can get. As we know, the average decline of a bear market is 30%. But we also know that the most recent bear market declines have been closer to 50%.

You don't allow your car, home, health, life, or even your RV to go uninsured. So the perma-bull and the growling bear should insure their investments and retirement against loss as well.

Time is your friend; impulse is your enemy.

Trading the Trends 297

Chapter 25

Averages, Oscillators, & Trinkets

Trading the Trends uses defined tactics for drawing the trend and channel lines, and also encompasses the use of simple moving averages. Specifically, we have included the 50 and the 200 DMA in our examples. However, as a personal choice, some traders use a 120 DMA either by itself or along with other moving averages. See Figure 20-1 below.

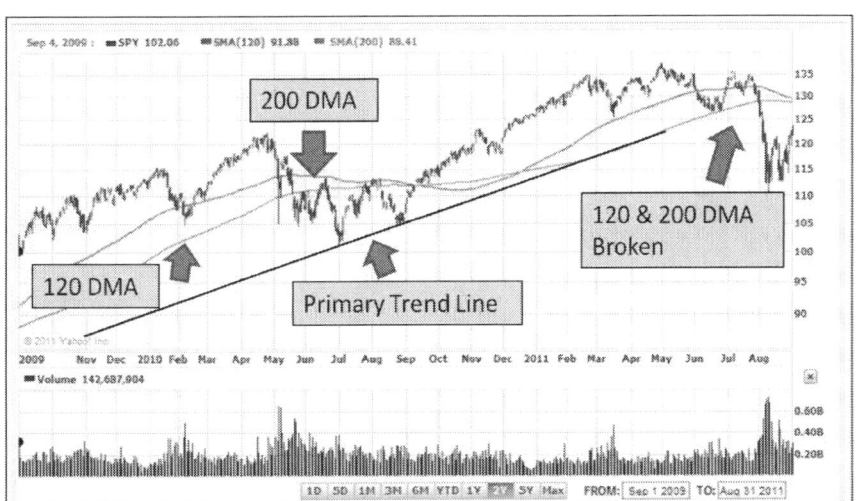

Figure 20-1

As you can see, the 120 DMA and the 200 DMA track the trend of the stock a little differently.

©Copyright McAllen Publishing

If I had extended the primary trend line in this example it would have covered the 120 DMA exactly as the stock traded down to touch it and then later broke below it. In this example, the stock broke the 200 DMA prior to breaking the trend or the 120 DMA. That is not always the case, as it can break one or the other first depending on their location at the time.

I would suggest using either of these moving averages or both if you prefer. They are both very effective to use in conjunction with the trend and channel lines. Moving averages are based on price and volume. These are the two things that matter. Charles Dow recognized it more than 100 years ago, and it is just as true today.

The market is a zero-sum game. For every buyer there is a seller, and vice versa. A market advance cannot take place unless buyers put their money on the table, and there are more of them, or more money, than there are sellers. A decline will happen when buyers become sellers and are taking their money off the table. The volume in each instance will tell you how serious the advance or decline really is.

Our trading examples have not included the use of Bollinger Bands, Fibonacci, or any trading software. We use simple trend lines, channel lines, technical analysis, and moving averages.

Let me explain.

The Perfect Indicator?

Investors and technicians often search through countless investing books looking for the one indicator that reliably predicts the market. Should you decide to try a new method of understanding the market or some new indicator, heed my admonition:

When you evaluate all the technical indicators, don't lose track of the general concept on which each indicator is based.

Those concepts are the important points. If you pay too much attention to the fine details and the intricate wiggles of some indicator, you often lose sight of the big picture. Any indicator is just there to help you see the larger story the market is telling; don't give that indicator some magical importance beyond that. Indicators are just tools to help you see what is happening in various segments and sectors of the market. After trading for more than 25 years, I have learned that there isn't a perfect indicator. You will not find it. But there is also a weakness in searching through all the indicators and something to warn you about.

Obscuring the Obvious

Probably more than half of the technical market indicators are oscillators of one kind or another. I find oscillators far overrated. I never use them because I found that they are a form of esoteric mathematics that often prevents a person from seeing what is happening.

Using them often encourages a person to put something more into the market than is really there. If you can't see what is happening in the market, you won't discover a deeper truth by studying an oscillator; it can't tell you anything more than the original statistic on which the oscillator is based. I know I'm being overly critical here, but I'm trying to make a point.

For example, many oscillators are calculated from the advance-decline line. The advance-decline line is simply the difference between two numbers: the number of stocks advancing and the number declining. There is no greater truth buried in this number. The creation of the advance-decline line was originally intended simply to pinpoint market divergences, periods when the popular averages were going up while most stocks were going down. That's all.

Then people started taking moving averages of the advance-decline line. They began subtracting one moving average from another moving average and plotting this line. They started adding these differences and plotting the sum. They even started looking for trend lines of this measure. You can see how this process can slowly remove a person from a simple and direct observation of the market.

Doing this is a little like taking a simple equation, such as $1 + 1 = 2$, squaring it, taking the fifth root, and then adding 3 to it. Doing more to this number won't give you any greater truth than the original simple equation of $1 + 1 = 2$. It is unnecessary mathematical complexity to find some deep meaning underneath all the data, but there isn't any.

That is not the direction to proceed to discover what the stock market is going to do. Just by looking at the advance-decline line, I can tell you what any oscillator will look like. The oscillators are calculated from the advance-decline line, so they can't tell you anything that the line itself can't tell you. With many oscillators, technical analysts are simply bottling up tap water, adding bells, whistles, and a little mystery, and selling it as a magical potion. It's just plain tap water.

The bottom line is most indicators use some intricate way to attempt to determine future market direction when in fact the indicator itself is based one way or another on price and volume. And price and volume are displayed on a chart for you to see and make rational and logical decisions that can include other factors as well, such as market sentiment or the overall economy. Remember that the market is just sometimes unpredictable. So instead of searching for some indicator that will tell you what you *want to hear*, remember the saying:

"When in doubt, stay out."

During these unpredictable periods, investors and technicians often become frantic trying to figure it out. They investigate all sorts of wave theories and indicators looking for some subtle clue. They often start stretching things and magnifying unimportant indications out of proportion trying to find the answer.

However, the market at that moment is simply saying it is unpredictable. So don't push it. It's telling you, "Be careful - this is a major trap." At those moments, it is best to back away and say, "I don't know," and then wait until the picture becomes clear and conclusive.

Before every major move, the market will tell you very clearly what is happening. The indication is never some obscure wiggle in an indicator. When it happens, you'll see it, and you'll know it.

Trading software

Throughout this book I have used simple candlestick charts (free on Yahoo) for two reasons.

1. To show the average investor that expensive charting tools or trading software is not necessary to make wise decisions, recognize opportunities, and be successful.
2. Because *'simple'* works.

To be successful you only need to make good, informed decisions based on proven techniques that have worked in all types of markets. Although some envision simply having a computer recognize opportunity and make the trade while they sit back and watch the money roll in, that is simply not going to happen. If it were that simple the computer programmer would have a 'golden-egg' and every reason on the planet not sell or share that golden egg with anyone.

My advice is this: Instead of wasting time trying to find an easy way, spend your time learning what works. It's not the *tricks of the trade* that matter. It's the knowledge.

> ***"If an individual learns the trade -***
> ***Then they don't need the tricks."***
> **~Fred McAllen**

Save Donkey Kong for the weekend. Pretty colors and fast fingers don't build account balances; understanding price behavior and the market does. So don't waste money on trading software that is incapable of rational and logical thought. Instead, learn technical market analysis.

> **"The average man doesn't wish to be told that it is a bull or a bear market. What he desires is to be told specifically which particular stock to buy or sell. He wants to get something for nothing. He does not wish to work. He doesn't even wish to have to think."**
> **~Jesse Livermore**

Chapter 26

Your Strategy

We have covered many trading examples, strategies, and experiences. Learning to make informed decisions when entering or exiting a trade or investment is vital to your success. At the same time, having a strategy and a plan to enter and exit each trade separates the winners from the losers. But first, you must decide what kind of trader or investor you will be.

Over the years, things have changed markedly in the stock market. Since the mid-1980s, the markets have been moving up and down rapidly. Prices have been highly volatile. While it may once have taken six months for the price of a stock to move from $30 to $40, such moves today can occur in a matter of several days and, on occasion, in a single day. This situation has, by necessity, created many opportunities over short periods of time.

Individuals who once considered themselves investors have now become traders. And some have even become day traders in order to capitalize on the often-large intraday price swings in many stocks.

In practice, there are only a few considerations in determining whether one wants to be a trader or an investor. There are tax advantages to investing as opposed to trading. But if the amount of money you can make as a trader is larger and faster than what you can make as an investor, then the larger tax may be worth paying.

At the same time, the long-term investor must also consider the fact that paying taxes might very well be better than not having the money. Meaning, many investors would likely have paid the taxes on the gains they had in 2000 or 2007 at the market highs instead of watching possibly 50% of their money evaporate in the market declines. Even Uncle Sam takes less than 50%.

Every investor or trader must develop his or her own trading or investing strategy. You may decide to use the predictive approach. This would mean entering and exiting trades earlier with slightly more risk. Or, you may have a confirming personality and choose to take a confirming approach to investing. Waiting for confirmation would most generally have you entering and exiting later, and less often. Then there are those who want to stay fully invested, but want to protect their account balance from huge losses.

For the most part, everyone falls into one of those types of traders and investors. Some long-term investors may only make two or three trades a year, or may stay fully invested during long-term primary trends that last for several years.

He/she may decide to stay invested through major declines and protect the capital using options.

The short-term investor or trader may make one or more trades a month depending on the movement of the market at the time. Capturing five to ten percent gains in short periods of time can be more risky, but the potential gains are high as well.

Options should always be considered when developing your strategy. Depending on your style of investing or trading, options can be a minor or a major part of your plan.

Regardless what plan fits your personality, or which one you eventually decide to use, they all have one thing in common.

"Limit your risk and protect your capital"

If you do not protect your capital, you may have no capital left to protect. Many learned this the hard way during the last two bear markets. Although those losses are certainly unfortunate, the use of a trend line could have prevented financial disaster for many.

Define your Strategy

When you define the strategy and plan you will follow, write it down. *Write it in stone if necessary*. Having a plan to follow is that important. Sticking to it is equally important. List each step, such as when you will enter, when you will exit, your maximum loss, and every aspect of the trade. Be descriptive as to what you will do when your investment breaks support, or breaks out above resistance. And make sure your plan limits your risk at all times.

In every trade we have waited for the market to come to us. This takes patience, but it is very important. You cannot force your will upon the market. The right trade setup will present itself very clearly. You won't have to look at daily charts to try to find some little wiggle in the trading range to justify an entry point you might want. The truth is, if you have to look that close, it's not there.

Closing the Losers

When the trend changes or the market simply goes against you, get out. Stay true to your predefined strategy and let your stop loss do the work. You must get out when your investment or trading method says to do so! Even if you get out and the market takes another turn and proves that you would have been alright to stay in, that's fine. There will be other opportunities. Just be patient and wait.

I want to share some general market and trading knowledge I've learned through experience. Use these bits of information to your advantage.

MARKET WISDOM

When investing or trading:

- Always use a stop loss

Never risk your money without first knowing how much you are willing to risk and use a stop loss to limit that risk. Being stopped out early does not mean you are a bad investor or trader. It only means you entered at the wrong time or the market went against you.

A loss gives you new information to work with. A new level that you now know may be either new support or resistance, or the market is searching for a support level lower than you anticipated. This is new information; use it to your advantage. A broken support level will likely be future resistance. Plan your next trade accordingly.

- Forget the news. Instead, watch for support, resistance, and trends.

You and I are not smart enough to know how news will affect the price of a stock or the overall market. It may be great news and the price declines or bad news and the price advances. The chart already knows and reflects it. Whatever it is, the market has already discounted it. For instance, one day while watching the market trade, overall it was only down slightly, but I noticed the banks were getting hit badly. Some had fallen that day to the tune of 3% or more. There was no news that would warrant such a decline. Well, the next morning I scan the headlines and see the Government is about to file a lawsuit seeking billions of dollars from many of the banks for their part in the housing and mortgage financial crisis.

The point here is two-fold. First, someone obviously knew beforehand what was coming or highly suspected it. It would certainly not have been a coincidence that the bank stocks got a three to five percent haircut only hours before the release of a news story. Secondly, at the same time, the market was discounting information that had yet to be released to the public.

- If you have to look for some subtle wiggle in the chart pattern to try to get it to make sense, it isn't there.

Price has memory. Look to see what the price did the last time it hit a certain level. Watch when a favorite stock or the market returns to a price level. Chances are it will do it again. The prior action will likely be repeated.

- Be the first in and out of the profit door.

Take their money before they take yours. Always be ready to pounce on the crowd's ill-advised decisions, poor judgment, and bad timing. Holding through major declines and corrections will make you broke, and keep you there.

- Buy the second low. (higher low)
- Sell the second high. (short sale – lower high)

The first test of a new high should fail. The first test of a new low should succeed. Watch for a breakout or breakdown the next time around.

- Buy the first pullback from a new high.
- Sell the first bounce from a new low.
- Buy at support.
- Sell at resistance.

Trading the Trends

When you walk into a wall you find resistance. Price has only two choices when it reaches a barrier: continue forward or reverse.

- Short rallies, not selloffs.

When markets drop, short sellers get ready to cover, making this a terrible time to execute new short sales. Wait until they ignite a bounce or squeeze and get shaken out at higher prices. Then jump in quietly while no one is watching.

- Don't chase a trade or catch a falling knife.

Profitable trades find the right entries, while losing trades chase the wrong ones.

- Avoid the market open. They see you coming.

The best strategy when the market opens is to sit on your hands. The professionals thrive off the unsuspecting. It is a time when the novices are frantically buying or selling and you don't want to get caught in a whipsaw. Always use the closing prices for your decisions. Those are the ones that matter. The close tells you where the real money is. The serious money will either stay in the market or it will sell out and go home. Market strength can be seen when the market trades higher during the day and closes at or near the high. That tells you the buyers are serious and they are staying in the market. On the flip side, when the market sells off during the day and into the close, the money is coming off the table. They do not have the conviction to stay, so they sell out to keep their money safe.

©Copyright McAllen Publishing

- Don't confuse a late afternoon rally with market strength.

During a weak market a late afternoon rally is nothing but a Day Traders' short-covering rally. If the market has sold off all day, the Day Traders will cover their short positions before the close. Don't worry, they aren't giving up. They will likely sell short again on the first bounce tomorrow morning.

- The trend is your friend.

Strong stocks get stronger and weak stocks get weaker. A strong market will continue in its direction until it changes, and those changes are a process that takes time. Weak stocks seldom fall for just one day. So don't jump in at the first low thinking you are buying at the bottom. Wait for confirmation, such as a higher low.

- Never toss a coin into the fountain hoping your dreams will come true.

Successful investing or trading is not about hopes and dreams. Plan your trade and trade your plan. If you were right, learn from it. If you were wrong, learn from it as well.

- Trade with the trend, not against it.

Go with the money flow. Draw trend lines and channels to predict where the next big move will occur. Then trade with the wind to your back. The market is trying to tell you something...listen.

©Copyright McAllen Publishing

- Know the price that violates the pattern.

Keep both risk and reward in sight at all times. Look for entries where the price must move only a short distance to show that the trade was a mistake. Then look the other way to find a profit target and apply this math to every opportunity.

- Limit execution to positions with low risk and high profit potential.

Then update analysis regularly. Control risk before seeking reward. Once you are in a profitable position it is too easy to count your chickens before they hatch. Continue to watch support and resistance levels and move your stop loss accordingly. By following your trading plan, when your chickens do hatch, you may wind up with a full coop.

- The markets have no intention of giving money to those who do not earn it.

Big losses rarely come without warning. You have no one to blame but yourself. The chart, the trend, and the moving average told you to leave. When a market is topping out and rolling over, there are always warning signs and time to get out. Don't ignore what it's saying. If you have a good gain, don't get greedy. Take what the market gives you and be satisfied.

- Bulls live above the 200 DMA, bears live below.

Trading the Trends

The 200 DMA divides the investing world in two. Bulls and greed live above the 200 DMA, while bears and fear live below. Sellers eat up bounces and rallies by short selling below this line, while buyers come to the rescue above it.

- When in Rome – do as the Romans do.

When the market is in bear territory, use its actions to your advantage. When the market is in bull territory, then run with the bulls.

- Enter in mild times and exit in wild times.

Don't count on the agitated crowd for your trading signals. Execute new trades in narrow trading range days at support or resistance whenever possible. Wide range trading days when the market is swinging numerous points up and down, in and out of positive territory, is a time to observe. Maybe just go fishing. Enter on mild days close to support or resistance.

- Trends rarely turn on a dime.

Reversals build slowly, at both the top and the bottom. Reversals are a process, not an event. Many investors are as stubborn as mules and take a lot of pain before they admit defeat and finally sell.

Conversely, short sellers are true disbelievers and won't cover without a fight. When the trend line, channel line, or moving average tells you to leave, then leave. Don't wait to see how big your loss can be. Let someone else risk their money while the market decides on its direction. Spend your time observing and looking for the next low risk entry.

These are simple market observations and trading rules that have held true for decades. The market doesn't always go up, and it doesn't always go down. It is what it is. You now have the tools to profit in any market environment. Use this knowledge to your advantage.

Remember, the market gives and it takes away. But by implementing a sound investing and trading plan, sticking to it, and using what you've learned, you can avoid the *'takes away'* side of the market.

> **People who are high-level investors are not concerned about the market going up or going down because their knowledge will allow them to make money either way.**

Conclusion

We have covered a lot of territory. I trust this has been a true learning experience. In closing, just remember there are no guarantees. The market may rise over the next twenty years, or it may decline. We may live to see new market highs, and again, it may not make new highs in our lifetime. There are no guarantees for the investor who blindly buys and holds, hoping the eggs they placed in a basket will magically produce a chicken farm someday.

We don't know what the market will do tomorrow or next week. But we do know the market will continue to advance and decline as it moves through the cycles it has followed for more than a century. Those cycles are the Trend Trader's bread and butter. We don't have to depend or rely on a market advance in order to realize profit. We have the tools to make money in any market cycle.

But you must always trade and invest with a strategy and a plan. Every successful investor and trader can only take what the market gives, and should do so with humility, acceptance, and good humor. It may give you nothing or only a little today, but there will be other days.

So never set your goals to make a certain dollar figure on any one investment or trade and expect the market to react to your wishes. You will be sorely disappointed.

Always treat the market with great respect. Combine discipline, planning, and patience through every trading opportunity. The markets work to fool the majority at every turn. So don't try to predict what it will do tomorrow. Instead, look at the big picture, it's always much clearer. Use common sense and logic to make wise decisions. You will learn from those decisions and profit from them in the future.

Happy Trading,
Fred McAllen
fredmcallen.com

> "There is only one side to the stock market;....not the bull side or the bear side, but the right side. It took me longer to get that general principle fixed firmly in my mind than it did most of the more technical phases of the game of stock market speculation."
> ~Jesse Livermore

©Copyright McAllen Publishing

Other books by Fred McAllen:

Whether you are investing or trading in stocks, options, or even Mutual Funds, technical market analysis is imperative to success. Fred McAllen explains every aspect in detail.

You will learn:
• Candlestick charting used by all professionals
• How to pinpoint entries and exits
• When the pros are buying
• When they are selling

#1 Investing book on Amazon and Kindle.

The Investing Book an investor cannot do without.

Learn market history and a common sense approach To investing.
You will learn the good and Bad about:
• Buy and Hold
• The Best Six Months Strategy
• Options Strategy
• Moving Average Strategy
•And Much More - -
Most of all, you will become a well informed investor. A true learning experience.

Printed in Great Britain
by Amazon